SUBSIDIA BIBLICA

32

subsidia biblica — 32

JOHN J. KILGALLEN, S.J.

TWENTY PARABLES
OF JESUS
IN THE GOSPEL OF LUKE

EDITRICE PONTIFICIO ISTITUTO BIBLICO — ROMA 2008

ISBN 978-88-7653-637-3
© E.P.I.B. – Roma – 2008
Iura editionis et versionis reservantur

EDITRICE PONTIFICIO ISTITUTO BIBLICO
Piazza della Pilotta, 35 - 00187 Roma, Italia

TABLE OF CONTENTS

INTRODUCTION

Consider for a moment Jesus' Sermon on Mount according to Matthew's Gospel. In the first half of this Sermon, one finds a variety of Jesus' teaching methods. There are authoritative statements ("Amen I say to you…"), there are metaphors (you are the light, you are the salt), antithetical statements (you have heard it said, but I say to you), repetition (in the teaching regarding prayer, penance and almsgiving, one only need to change few elements in each paragraph to move from one activity to the other). Jesus used many forms of teaching to help his audience understand and remember his lessons.

The Parable

One of the most vibrant means Jesus employed to teach his wisdom was the parable. Ordinarily, a parable is a fictitious story with at least one element that represents the real world (some scholars would say that the ideal parable has only one point to make). However, in the ancient world of Jesus, the word *parable* can mean other than a story; it can refer to any type of comparison by which one uses the fictitious world to make clearer sense of the real world. For instance, such a simple literary device as metaphor falls under the name of parable; it is no story, but a phrase or word which illuminates the real by virtue of the fictitious. Consider the sentence: the Chicago Bears (a football team) are lions on defence. The Bears players are not actual lions, but they exhibit the toughness and fearsomeness of lions. When one hears them called 'lions', one understands that their real qualities are being explained by making them appear, fictitiously, as lions — and one understands from this fiction how feared are the Chicago Bears on defence. Such a comparison qualifies as a parable in the ancient world.

From our just-mentioned example, we understand that the word "parable" in itself makes clear that the parable can exist in a literary form other than story, e.g. a metaphor or simile. Parable comes from the Greek roots *para* and *bole*, meaning respectively 'along side' and 'placed' ('thrown'). These two Greek words together mean that 'one thing is placed beside another'; the purpose of placing one thing beside another is to make clearer one of those two things. A good synonym for 'parable' is 'comparison'. Thus, the hope of the speaker of the parable is that, having placed something fictitious next to something real (i.e. having compared something real with something fictitious), the meaning of the real will be clearer. Perhaps the purest parable story, that which has only one lesson, is the story that begins with "The kingdom of Heaven is like…"; an example of this is the parable: "the kingdom of Heaven is like a merchant's search for fine pearls; when he found one really valuable pearl, he went back and put up for sale all that he had and bought it." The speaker has placed the 'kingdom of Heaven' beside a 'really valuable pearl', and thereby has he made clearer the value of the kingdom of Heaven.

Luke's 20 parables — why these?

There are many metaphors and similes in the Gospel of Luke which, strictly speaking, qualify to be studied under the title of 'parable' or comparison. Our interest will be restricted to 20 parables, to 20 fictitious stories. (Note: in our Index or Table of Contents there are 17 parables indicated; this number 17 becomes 20 when we realize that two parables instead of one are treated in one place and three parables instead of one are treated in another place.) The reasons for this restriction to 20 are four.

First, these 20 stories are, by dint of history and liturgy and spiritual reading and meditation, supremely famous — consider just two parables, that of the Good Samaritan and that of the Prodigal Son (found only in Luke).

Second, a metaphor can be understood with a modicum of thought and/or a bit of reading, whereas these 20 parables demand quite a bit of reflection and a good amount of reading; this book tries to make these studies less onerous.

Third, one is asked to pay attention, when one tries to understand a parable, to the potential difference between what lesson Jesus means to draw from the parable, which Jesus gives in 30 AD, and what lesson Luke means to draw from the parable, when he chooses to tell it in 85 AD. If one does not pay attention to this distinction, one risks missing the meaning of the parable. Certainly, we will occasionally distinguish what Jesus intended for his audience from that which Luke intended for his audience, but only occasionally; it is hoped that the reader will get used to doing his for himself. Concretely, this last point, when applied to Luke, means constant attention not only to the parable in itself and as one can excise it from the context, but also to the context in which one finds the parable perfectly embedded in the Gospel by Luke. We will see how very often it is Luke's introduction to the parable or his general context which leads us to a meaning which is perhaps what Jesus did not directly intend in 30 AD, but which can be drawn from his parable for an audience of 85 AD, an audience which is quite different from that of Jesus. There is no sly trickery in this on Luke's part; it is just that a fictitious story in itself allows for more than one meaning, as the speaker (in this case, Jesus) knows. The value of the parable is its enlightenment of real life with God and neighbor; it is understandable that the audience of 30 AD can differ significantly from the audience of 85 AD. Just consider telling a story in 1950 AD and applying it to the realities of 2005 AD, or, what might be even more interesting, telling a story in 2005 AD and guessing how best it will be applied to the realities of 2060 AD! What one must realize is that all meaning that Luke intended as he re-told Jesus' parables is in agreement with the mind and intention of Jesus.

Fourth, the hope of this book is that, by carefully considering the 20 parables herein, one may have learned a kind of method by which to approach the literary world of the parable and the religious world of God as expressed in the text and context of the parables.

Four aspects of parables worthy of particular note:

First, there is a need to understand the parables of Jesus as they fit the lives of his hearers; that is, one must understand well the social, political, religious world of Palestine in 30 AD. We try to provide enough of this in this book to let one see how the parable squares with first-century Palestinian Jewish life.

Second, there are subdivisions of the term 'parable'. A particularly important subdivision for us is called 'exemplum', which means that, while we are given a fictitious story meant to enlighten the real world (hence a parable), the point of the parable-exemplum is limited to providing a fictitious moral example to be followed. Thus, the Good Samaritan, while a fictitious story, offers as its goal an example to follow.

Third, often Jesus comes across as Lord or Master; thus, in the Gospel we can expect him to command — and we are to obey. True, his commands are wise, but the form in which his wisdom reaches us is still very often that of command. But at times Jesus abandons this literary method and moves to another. In this other mode, he usually asks a question which calls on the audience, not himself, to judge what is right and wrong: "Which of you...?" Instead of a command, which assumes Jesus is right, it belongs to the audience to judge from its own experience what is right and wrong. Implicit in this kind of parable is the expectation of Jesus that, if you see where right and wrong exist in the fictitious example, you will have seen better what is right and wrong in the life with God.

Fourth, the parable must be told in such a way that the audience can find no error in the fictitious story; once one finds such an error, one may refuse to listen further to the speaker and says to himself, "Maybe he is speaking about his experiences, but he is not speaking about mine, so I leave him."

A concrete example: if at any point in his story regarding the Good Samaritan, a detail is incorrect, Jesus will lose his audience. Thus, if the action of the priest, the action of the Levite, the circumstances of danger on the road from Jerusalem to Jericho, the response of the Samaritan, the things necessary for the cure of the fallen man (e.g. wine and oil as curing agents) — if these details are considered impossible or outside the audience's experience, Jesus will lose his audience. That Jesus kept the interest of the audiences throughout his parables is testimony to the fact that Jesus understood his audiences, was well within every audience's experiences, and taught very well the lesson(s) to be gained from comparing a fictitious (but understandable) situation of their world to the real world of God and man.

Luke and his sources

Occasionally a person who reads one or other of the 20 parables discussed in this book will say to himself, "I have read this parable elsewhere, in Mark and/or Matthew". This observation is true: some of the parables in Luke are to be found also in Mark and/or Matthew. The question is: should we systematically compare what Luke says with Mark, the source of his material, or with Matthew, who often uses the same source Luke uses? On the one hand, a comparison is in order, for through comparison one sees in what ways Luke wants to tell the story differently from his sources, and so we arrive more surely at what Luke wanted to say. On the other hand, while the end-result of comparison to sources is good, it is a difficult and long study and sometimes hypothetical in its conclusions; though an admirable and profitable study in itself, it was not judged 'doable' in this book. More to the point, we can doubt that Luke's audience compared Luke with Mark or Matthew; rather, that audience more likely read the Gospel without reference to sources. This book is in part based on this mode of the first reader's experience: just read Luke and reflect on what he has presented. Later, it seems right to say, one can compare Luke to his sources, to see if any meaning in Luke's parables was missed.

   A most interesting fact is that 16 of our 20 parables occur in what is called Luke's Grand Insertion. The Grand Insertion is a block of material which in the Gospel extends from 9, 51 till 18, 14. This collection is generally recognized as coming neither from Mark nor from Q (a source Luke shared with Matthew, but not with Mark). It is a section devoted to teaching, once Jesus is "on the way to and through Jerusalem" (to sitting at God's right hand in readiness to be Judge of the world). The one parable that occurs before this Grand Insertion is that of the Sower and the Seed (Luke 8), which is a fundamental parable meant both to analyze reactions to Jesus' past assertions and to anticipate the reception Jesus' preaching will and will not receive in the following chapters; three parables occur after 18, 14, in that period when, with Jesus now close to Jerusalem, the thought of his departure and of final judgment looms large and merits enlightened teaching, through parables.

Our order of presentation of the 20 parables

We turn, then, to 20 parables of Luke's Gospel. The order in which the 20 parables are presented here means to respect the decision of Luke as to when each parable was to be read. The order of the parables, then, is not our statement of the order in which Jesus originally gave his parables, but the order is 'chronological' in accord with and out of respect for Luke's literary plan.

Together with each parable title are the verses which contain the parable. These verses are given without parentheses. Where there are verses given in parentheses, the parentheses mean to suggest verses which do not make up the parable itself, but are necessary, as context, to understand the parable.

1. THE SOWER AND THE SEED — LUKE 8, 5-8 (8, 4-15)

A Question of Context

The parable about the sower, the seed and various soils in which the seed is placed is interested in one thing: That the sower's seed knows a variety of results, that often the seed fails because of the soil which receives it, and how often the seed succeeds because of the good soil which receives it. This parable, the only one of our famous 20 which is given in Galilee, is both lengthy in itself and is followed by an equally lengthy interpretation of it; it is meant, then, to be a comment first of all on the reception of Jesus' preaching in Galilee, then an anticipation on all of his and the disciples' future preaching. Between the parable and its interpretation we have words of Jesus which center on 'the disciples and the others', the former being the ones to whom the mysteries of the Kingdom are explained, the latter being the ones to whom are given 'only parables'.

Since many of Jesus' parables are accompanied by his or Luke's interpretation, to say that we have a parable here with a subsequent interpretation seems to say nothing new. But there are some peculiarities to note here that make our parable + interpretation unique.

First, as preparation for the parable, we are told that a large crowd is accompanying Jesus, and at the same time the numbers swell as he is joined by a stream of people coming from the town he is passing; from another point of view, we know we have in our audience people who have been following Jesus devotedly (vv. 1-3) and others who can range from curious to inimical. Such a large audience is not customary when Jesus gives his parables. What Luke seems to be doing here is presenting an audience which corresponds to the breadth of the parable. There are all kinds of people here, each to respond to the teaching of Jesus in his own, welcoming or unwelcoming, way. Indeed, once we read the full event here (vv. 4-15), one perceives the implicit suggestion that this audience is not monolithic in its faith in Jesus, but that rather its variety of faith and non-faith in him is precisely what this parable describes — it is a parable whose audience represents the many people who have heard/responded to and will hear/respond to the teachings of Jesus.

Second, the conclusion to the parable is rather significant (He cried out, 'Let him who has ears, hear!'). It is a unique cry in a Gospel of many parables. It is a plea to the various people listening to him to find themselves in the parable. Everyone falls into a category of soil described in the parable. Jesus' call for a real 'hearing' is a call to recognize one's status and respond to what one recognizes about himself.

Third, we do find Jesus' interpretation of the parable, and it is a lengthy one, much longer than anything he offers elsewhere in the Gospel; it is unique.

Fourth, the interpretation does not follow immediately on his cry for attentiveness, but after a private meeting with his disciples. It is in this meeting that Jesus gives a very important clarification. This comment, a tightly expressed thought of Jesus which we must stretch out a bit, indicates the fact: to the disciples will be explained the mysteries of the kingdom of God, whereas to the 'rest', the kingdom will be expressed only in puzzling parables. Nowhere else is there a similar introduction to Jesus' interpretations of his parables.

The distinction, between those to whom the mysteries (i.e. the meaning or explanation of the mysteries) are given and those who receive these mysteries only in puzzling parables, pivots on the term 'to you'. That is, to disciples of Jesus, who are characterized by acceptance of and faith in him, will understanding of the parables be possible; only for them, once they basically have accepted Jesus as the center of the kingdom of God, can the parables be successfully unravelled and fully explained. Conversely, if one does not believe in Jesus, one has no key by which to understand the kingdom of God and its mysteries. To this person, now without faith in Jesus, Jesus draws on words of Isaiah to express the effect of his unbelief: he will 'look and not see, listen and not understand.' Again, the argument is: how can one hope to understand the mysteries, if he does not first believe in Jesus, about whom the parables speak? It is not a question of Jesus' speaking too ambiguously; it is a question of believing that he is at the center of the mysteries. Without conceding him that role, the mysteries cannot be understood. He alone is what gives clarity to the mysteries.

We should add that the word 'mysteries' here does not imply, as it often does in other literature, something one will never understand or know. Rather it means something that can (and will) be known only if one has the key which opens the door to making the mysteries intelligible.

No doubt, this story of 'you' and 'the others' takes on a more definite appeal when it is read, as in the case of Luke's Gospel, some 50 years after the experience of those who have been baptized in Christ and those who have refused. The story explains Jesus' encounters, successful and not, in his own generation, and also in the brief the history of faith and non-faith which has characterized the response to Christian preaching of the past half-century between Jesus and Luke.

A Presupposition of the Parable

We should know that the sowing that Jesus describes here was the actual way in which seed was sown in his time. Perhaps such an observation about sowing seed is unnecessary, but people have questioned this rather crude, apparently wasteful method of sowing seed. As the seed is tossed at the end of a field, inevitably some landed by the side of a road; similarly, not all rocks were so far away from the field that some seed might not land next to a rock or among rocks. Similarly there are enough weeds about and little soil among them, so that, again, there is seed that does not succeed in becoming what it should. These possibilities all existed in first-century farming. And yes, the growth from seed in good ground often seems too disproportionate to the tiny beginning that one can call it a 'hundredfold', but such it can be.

The Message of the Parable and a Critical Study of it

The parable is seen to contrast two states: that of a happy production and that of a frustrated or failed seed. What is central to the entire story is the quality of the land which receives the seed; there is never any change about the sower or about the seed. First, we are given three examples of the results of seed falling on unreceptive soil; then we are given one example of the results of seed falling on receptive soil. Scholars are divided as regards the point at issue here. There is no doubt that the constant theme is "the soils".

Some specialists, despite the disproportion between 3 and 1, think that it is in the final point of the parable that the message is to be found: thus, Jesus means to underline the assurance that seed will find good soil and will produce abundance — at least in some of the audience before him. This interpretation stresses the joy of successful seeding, particularly the value of good soil, no matter how many failures there may be elsewhere along the way.

Other scholars look to the disproportion mentioned above (3 to 1), and understand the parable to say that there will be many failures in seeding, though there is occasional success. This view stresses the failures of many soils to receive the seed. Is the parable meant to convey a message which is positive or one which is negative? If one thinks that the parable is positive, one can take a step forward to say that this parable prefigures a joyful harvest to flow from faith in Jesus, no matter what setbacks from poor soils might occur along his way; if one thinks the parable is negative, one can step forward to say that the parable prefigures the failures of Jesus' preaching to plant faith, and even serves as a threat or severe criticism to those who do not accept him.

A critical, literary study of the parable, vv. 5-8, has tried to separate the elements of the parable as Jesus gave it from accretions made to the parable by people, e.g. first and second generation Christian preachers, who used the parable in later situations — the supposition here is that there are such additions and, since Luke was an inheritor of traditions, the parable came to Luke's attention with them. In this study, the elements of accretion are such that, when they are removed, the resultant parable, though still made up of 3 negative examples against only 1 positive example, can more easily be seen as positive: there is simply less time given in the explanations for failure, so that one can more easily be impressed with the soil and the description that it produces such a bountiful growth. In short, the parable assures precious success of preaching amidst its often disappointing failures.

I believe that the majority of scholars think that the reality in which Jesus lived makes the parable a statement about both failure and success. Thus, it is difficult to choose 'either joy or sadness' as the purpose of the parable. One thing is for certain. No one would fault Jesus on his overall experience: there are and will be disciples and enemies, good soil and bad soil; in this light, it seems logical to conclude that he speaks about his total experience, without undue emphasis on the bad or the good. To repeat what was said earlier, he offers this description to his audience: let each find himself in it. Perhaps we have a parallel thought in Simeon's balanced words about Jesus: ""This child is destined to cause the falling and rising of many in Israel" (2, 34).

Let us repeat an important distinction here. In none of the four examples of sowing that we have given us is there any change in seed or sower as we move from one example to the next. The seed and sower retain a constant and positive value. It is the soil which offers potential failure or success. There is at the moment little clarity (clarity comes later through Jesus' interpretation), though we can make suggestions, about the spiritual meanings intended by 'soil at the beaten-down road' 'soil on rocky ground', 'soil too shallow to allow roots to take hold', nor do we have precise description of what constitutes 'good ground'. The point here for the audience is not so much the detailed identification of each of the four examples, but the fact that, yes, there is good and bad soil — which are you?

One is very tempted to read Jesus for sower and his message for seed (it is possible to think of God as sower, and, in a later time, the Christian preacher who preaches both Jesus and his message); but neither Jesus nor Luke has revealed this — that is, neither introduction nor conclusion to the parable is concerned to identify explicitly the sower and seed. Again, concentration is on the soil - where does one find good soil?

A literary link: the question of the disciples (vv. 9-10)

The disciples ask Jesus for the meaning of 'this parable'. We have already emphasized that the key word here is 'disciples'. They are the content of the "you" whom Jesus addresses. They, because believers in Jesus, have the essential element by which to understand this and any parable; the 'others', non-believers in Jesus, no matter how hard they try to see and hear, will never understand this or any other parable. Could they understand something of the parable? Yes, they could. But they will never understand its profound meaning for their salvation, if they do not first believe in Jesus, if they are not 'his disciples'.

Jesus does not say to his disciples in private that because you believe in me, I will no longer speak to you in parables; but they will be able to understand the parables because of their faith. The continued speaking in parables will also be a constant form of communication with the non-believer. At stake, then, is not different modes of speech for different groups, but the difference between a believer and a non-believer; the former will be able, eventually, as the Gospel and Acts explain, through the influence of the Spirit, to interpret the parables correctly, while the latter who does not believe will always fail to understand the meaning of these parables which in fact are centered on Jesus. The believer, in these verses, is another way of saying 'the good earth' in which the seed has been planted. In him will understanding of the mysteries, as well as good deeds, grow.

Put another way, we compare Luke to his source, Mark; we see that in Luke is missing a precious statement of Jesus to his disciples: if you do not understand this parable (of the sown seed), how will you understand any of the other parables? This statement shows the fundamental reality this parable means to describe: the 'soils' will be the reason which make possible all and any further comprehension of the mysteries Jesus will teach. Yes, this sentence is missing in Luke, but not its meaning. Its meaning is in the distinction between 'disciple' and 'the rest'. The disciple, the good soil, is the one who, because of his faith, will be open to comprehend all else that Jesus will teach. Luke decided that he did not need Mark's verse, because his own verse ('you' and 'the rest') contained the idea: without faith, without being the good soil which has received the seed, one cannot hope to plumb the depths of meaning in Jesus' parables.

An example is, perhaps, in order. Jesus will give a parable to the effect that the kingdom of God is similar to a situation in which a man discovers a pearl of great price, and then sells all he has so that he may return to buy, or possess, the pearl. Certainly this parable is intelligible, as can be seen from the fact that everyone who hears it will praise the man who sells all in order to have something worth more than all he possessed previously. One can also interpret it with the understanding of traditional Judaism: serve God and Him alone, and the Kingdom is yours. But who understands 'selling of all else' (in order to possess the fabulous pearl, the kingdom of God) consists in faith in Jesus? Who will understand how to have 'the pearl of great price'? Only the person who believes in Jesus (and not just obedience to God) will have it, for only through him and his teaching can one enter the kingdom of Heaven. Only through understanding Jesus' role in one's having the great pearl will one fully understand the kingdom of Heaven.

The interpretation of the parable of the seed sown in various soils (vv. 11-15)

As mentioned, Jesus is talking here, not about a variety of seeds, but about a variety of soils. The seed is always the same: his preaching, or the preaching about him. Again, there is only one example of a successful sowing: the earth in this case is described, without further definition, as 'beautiful and good'; actually, this phrase, 'beautiful and good' was the description in the Greek world of the perfect human being, which is a harmony of external beauty with internal nobility. This description would make sense particularly to a Greek audience who cherished this ideal. For Jesus, it means the soil, perfectly prepared (which includes faith in Jesus), which receives the word of God and so produces a rich harvest.

If the parable in itself seemed more interested in the three soils which did not receive the seed than in the one soil which did, the present explanation of the parable stresses this 'imbalance'. The three examples are now explicit about the causes for the seed's failure to take solid hold; apparently, this explanation of the parable, limited to a triad of soils, means to concentrate heavily on the many causes of failure.

Corresponding to the three soils which fail to produce the expected hundredfold are these threats:

1. the Devil
2. not sufficiently deep roots to survive such opposition as trial or temptation
3. anxieties and wealth and the pleasures of life

A. *The Devil*

The 'Devil' is cited here as an explanation as to why some do not become believers (upon reflection, however, within the theology found in parts of the New Testament he has a role to play in the second and third causes, too). The explicit role of the Devil, apart from demon possession, is rarely seen in the writings of the New Testament; yet the belief in his enmity toward God is a given in the Old Testament and clearly a background thought and an experience witnessed in the testing of Jesus and in the demonic attacks on human beings in the New Testament. The Devil is the explanation for those people who resisted Jesus from the beginning, in whom there was not the slightest chance for the seed to grow. Thus, this case is not that of one who, as below, has the beginnings of faith. This case is that of those who had none; their total opposition is laid here, not to free will, but to the power which means to destroy God. Note that there is no attempt to describe what we often refer to as the psychological state which makes faith impossible.

B. *Trial or temptation*

The mention of 'trial' or 'temptation' particularly anticipates specific moments in the Gospel of Luke, particularly the fleeing of the disciples at Jesus' capture and death; in the Garden, Jesus had warned them to pray that 'they not enter into temptation' and so avoid this testing. Judas would be another, particular example of a failure to resist temptation against failing. No doubt, there were other examples of failure to keep one's faith which were known from the time of Jesus to Luke's time; thus, the poor soil, which was enough to accept the roots of faith, could not keep the faith in times of trial and temptation. Ananias and Saphira, in Acts 5, are examples of believers who lost their lives because they had not resisted temptation. The context for a number of writings, within and outside the New Testament, is persecution; the documents are written to bolster faith during these trials. If persecution and its challenge was part of the general life of the 1st-century churches, it is not surprising that the subject is brought up specifically here.

C. *Anxieties, wealth, pleasures*

Such references as 'anxieties and wealth and the pleasures of life' are a concern of Jesus throughout his preaching. The anxiety that concerns him is the state of an individual who looks to himself as the sole source of maintaining and developing life — he does not believe that God, his Father, will maintain and further his life. Inevitably, goes the thinking, a creature will always look to a god for stability, life and happiness. If one looks for 'final, essential' stability of life, the question then is: Who is my God?

Once one thinks he will find salvation apart from God, one's efforts turn to what one thinks to be the source(s) of life — often summed up in the word 'wealth'. Jesus does not deny the value of bread and all it stands for in the continuance of life, for the human being is not self-sustaining, but depends on many things from outside himself for continued life. But Jesus will argue strenuously that confidence only in bread cannot assure one of life. If bread be the sole source of life, one is enslaved to it as to one's sole 'lifeline'. One's energies and efforts will be given over to the search for wealth, the only source, one is convinced, of life. The call of death is a stark reminder that God, not bread, is the one who controls the length of life, as well as the life hereafter. To believe that someone or something, like wealth, can do all that God can do is to make that 'something', that wealth one's God, the means by which I live 'forever'. At the same time, this total commitment to wealth as my savior cannot but deny God's self-definition, Father of us. To call God Father, yet look elsewhere for the source of our existence is a contradiction which only ends in denying that He merits to be called 'our Father'. All of which comes to the ever-present question: 'who is my source of life, who is God for me'?

The 'pleasures of life' are universally recognized to be powerful means to corrupt ideals and religious faith. The satisfaction in them tends to make a person think that his happiness lies in them; any arduous demand of ideal or of faith challenges belief simply because one thinks he has found his joy (or will one day gain it) without the demands and sacrifices inherent in this faith. He needs nothing but pleasure to provide happiness, and so avoids suffering. If wealth can serve as source of life, so pleasures can serve as unending causes of happiness. In neither case does one need God or, specifically, a savior. Money or pleasure gives me all I want; I only need them all the time — and nothing or no one else. The people who think this way are soils in which the call to faith in Jesus and to repentance in order to enter the Kingdom is meaningless, soils in which faith will drop no productive roots.

All these 'soils' are in the experience of Jesus, but they are also in the experiences of many of his followers and missionaries throughout the 50 years between Jesus' preaching and Luke's Gospel. Some specialists think it is the church, on the basis of its experience, that has described the unproductive soils and given prominence, in its interpretation, to the failures to believe or hold to belief. This opinion might be right, but it is difficult, in the light of the Gospel narrative, to think that these soils were not in evidence also through the public life of Jesus, where refusal and contestation, for a variety of reasons, was clearly real.

Conclusion

The parable of the seed and the soils occurs a third of the way through the Gospel. As such, it can be seen as something of an analysis of Jesus' preaching and healing experiences in the first third of the Gospel, and a guide to the many times in the future when people will reject him or accept him. While it is often the case, particularly in Luke-Acts, where one is introduced to the Divine as cause of things, this parable assigns the causes of success and failure to the Devil; causes, too, are trials and temptations, and anxieties and money and pleasures of this world. One cannot fail to recognize Jesus' use of the Devil as a source of non-belief; this parable is one of many passages, here and elsewhere in the New Testament, where teachings make use of apocalyptic world structures — the God of good against the power of evil — as the most profound explanations for the good and evil in the world. Jesus himself serves as an example of the good soil in that he rejected temptation by three statements (cf. Luke 4, 1-12) that identified a) his belief in what (i.e. Who) will preserve forever and enhance his life, b) his firm conviction that only Yahweh deserves the reverence and obedience owed to God, and c) his extreme confidence in God's love for him. Eventually, before his capture and death (cf. Luke 22, 39-46), Jesus will repeat that his choice in life is always dictated by his Father's will, not his own. Indeed, his life of reverence and obedience makes intelligible to believers Jesus' life is the life that best reflects the truths of the many parables he gives.

In sum, to those who believe, all is made clear; to those who do not believe, the significance of the parables will always remain unknown, for it is faith in Jesus that makes understanding of the parables truly successful. But even more fundamental: belief in Jesus is the only way to understanding the meanings of the parables; without faith, the parables remain 'mysteries'.

2. THE GOOD SAMARITAN (LUKE 10, 30-35 [25-37])

First observation

As is clear from the designation above, the actual parable of the Good Samaritan runs through verses 30-35. But the parable is embedded within a discussion between Jesus and a lawyer (i.e. someone who is by profession an interpreter of the demands of the Mosaic Law and its traditions). We have another literary form than parable before and after the parable: dialogue. Both parts of the dispute with the lawyer must be considered (What must I do? Who is my neighbor?), so that the meaning of the parable, as Luke wants it interpreted, can be understood. Such a consideration will follow shortly, but first a bit of history.

The history behind the parable

The animosity between most Jews and most Samaritans in the time of Jesus was very strong; at various times they even hated each other. Why that was so is understandable from history, which follows:

A. From 921 BC to 722 BC

David forcibly united the Twelve Tribes into a kingdom called, fittingly, the Kingdom of David; he was succeeded by his son, Solomon, who even further developed the unified Kingdom. However, the son of Solomon who succeeded his father on the throne, created enough virulent opposition (increased taxation was one bitter royal imposition) that the northern two-thirds of the Kingdom rebelled against the southern one-third (with Jerusalem as its capital), and so two Kingdoms came into being. The northern kingdom was called variously in history: Israel, or the Northern Kingdom, or Samaria. The southern kingdom carried the name of Judea, or the Southern Kingdom. A major irritant between these two groups of Hebrews was the new temple built by the Jews of Samaria — a direct challenge to the renowned temple built by Solomon and considered by his generation (and the composers of the Old Testament) to be the true and only temple of God. The Jews of the Southern Kingdom continually considered the Kingdom of the North, Samaria, to be heretical. Obviously and conversely, the Samaritan Jews thought the southerners to be heretical. This situation continued for two-hundred years; neither kingdom had any love or respect for the other.

B. *From 722 BC to Jesus' time*

In 722 BC Assyria was the major power in the Middle East. As one might expect, Assyria turned its eye to the conquest of Israel and it defeated the Northern Kingdom, Samaria, in 722/721 BC; the Assyrians failed, or decided not to conquer the Southern Kingdom, Judea. The custom of Assyria was to move conquered peoples out of their homeland and into areas of the Assyrian kingdom which were totally new to them; similarly, the Assyrians filled up the newly depopulated area with people who had not known this land. Thus, the Northern Kingdom or Samaria became a territory very predominantly inhabited by non-Jews, a pagan people who "knew nothing of Yahweh". Were there Jews living there, those left over from the giant deportation of Jews out of Samaria? Yes, there were. But this Samaria, almost totally pagan, was odious to those who lived in Judea, who believed, not in pagan gods which came with these foreigners, but in the one, true God of Heaven and Earth.

Now, there is another side to this story. Samaritans exist today, perhaps only about 600 in our world, but they do exist. Their side of the story is, put simply, that they are the true and legitimate descendants of Abraham, Isaac and Jacob; the Jews of Judea are not. The Samaritans trace their lineage directly to Eli, the father of the great prophet Samuel (10th Century BC); for these Samaritan people, Jews descended from

Abraham, the Kingdom of Judea was the false and heretical kingdom. The true temple of Yahweh was to be found in their territory, in Bethel, and not in Jerusalem. These people practiced the true worship; the Jews of Judea did not.

As in the pre-Assyrian period, so ever after, there was no love lost between the people who inhabited the North (whether they be Jewish or non-Jewish) and those who lived in the South.

As a certain point in time and because of the decisions of conquering powers, the North and the South (Samaria and Judea) were divided into three parts: the southern third of the land was still called Judaea, the middle section of the land was called Samaria, and the northern third of the country was called Galilee. It is into this world that Jesus is born. The Samaria and Judaea of Jesus' time still maintained animosity towards each other. Jews from Galilee were afraid for their lives to pass through Samaria to get to Jerusalem, though such a route was the most direct and easiest. In the run of centuries between the Assyrian conquest and the time of Jesus there were certain events which were very public tragedies and exacerbated the contempt each group had for the other.

All of which adds up to the fact that when Jesus tells his parable of a Samaritan who cares for a Jew with such thorough care, he is describing a situation which few of his listeners in Judea wanted or liked to hear. A Samaritan saved the life of a Jew? If ever a parable strained Jewish credibility, it was this one; who among the Jews could put up with a suggestion so favourable to a Samaritan, and that at the cost to priest and Levite?

The priest and the Levite in Jesus' time

An essential of Israelite life was the worship of God in the Temple of Jerusalem. The number of sacrifices there was enormous. Just recall that every day, twice a day, there was a very formal worship ceremony: music and singing, offerings of bread, oil and wine and two lambs characterized each sacrifice. One can only imagine the number of offerings, of official designation or private gifts, that occurred all through the year in Jerusalem; indeed, we remember that all male, adult

Jews were to go to Jerusalem to worship three times a year at the great feasts: Passover, Pentecost and Tents; how many sacrifices were offered at those times!

To care for the Temple worship there were, in the time of Jesus, an estimated seven or eight people called 'Chief Priests'; they served under the most important person in Israel, the High Priest. These seven or eight people were the only priests who functioned as priests all year round. So enormous was the activity in the Jerusalem Temple that the High Priests and Chief Priests responsible for the worship in the Temple had to have daily help. So came into being those called priests. It has been suggested that there were 7200 priests available at different times of the year for Temple service; each priest took his designated time and task. At most, a priest functioned as a priest for eight weeks a year; obviously, he had to have another job to support himself and his family for the rest of the year. That Jesus describes a priest (and a Levite, as well) as 'on his way from Jerusalem' suggests that the priest has finished his designated service in Jerusalem and is on his way home. Perhaps the priest best-known to us today is Zachary (Zachariah), the father of John the Baptist. Recall that the angel Gabriel appeared to Zachary while the latter was helping with the worship emanating from the altar of incense, an altar found in the middle of the three rooms that made up the Temple.

The Levite, with a long history like the priesthood, functioned, like the priest, only about eight weeks a year in the Temple of Jerusalem. His task is best described as the musician and singer who accompanied every official, public sacrificial sanctuary. The Levites numbered, one guesses, about 9600; each of them, like the priest, will have his designated times to be present in the Temple. He, too, 'is on his way down from Jerusalem', returning home, it is presumed, to resume his year-round job.

The function of the priest and the Levite in Jesus' parable

The most common explanation of the priest and the Levite in this parable is that they, among all Israelites, represent the Law of Moses. Though they were by no means defined as experts in interpreting that

Law (Scribes were the experts), in a practical sense they stood for, or represented that Law. From this description, one would expect from priest and Levite an excellent observance of the Law of Moses and traditions authoritatively derived from it. One of the teachings of the Mosaic Law was that a Jew is not to touch a dead body. Indeed, many cultures had many prohibitions of this kind, presumably rooted in a fear of diseases from 'unclean' things. If one touched a dead body, he should be purified; otherwise, he was forbidden to enter into worship God with his community — he will contaminate the others.

That the priest and Levite do not touch the body, or even go close to it, is a sign that they know the Law of Moses about touching dead bodies and obey it. For this they should be praised, one would think.

The Jew left half-dead

As Jesus tells his story, the fallen Jew is not dead, but 'left for dead', 'half-dead'. Should the priest and Levite have recognized the true condition of their neighbour and thus know that they can touch him, because he is only half-dead? While the question can be asked, the answer seems to lie, not in the true state of the man (which we readers know from Jesus), but in the perception of two people who are so dedicated to the Law that they will not proceed any further, once they judge that touching the man would break the Law of Moses: this means that they no doubt thought that the man was dead, though the storyteller describes him as half-dead.

The problem of the conduct of priest and Levite

The listener to Jesus' story was expected to understand and even praise the priest and the Levite for their obedience to the Law. Fidelity to the will of God was the hallmark of the good Jew. What will be at stake, however, is the question of the relationship among the Laws of God. Moses makes clear that God does not want a dead body touched. But Moses also makes clear that the supreme law of God is two-fold: love of God and love of neighbour. By saying that love of God and love of neighbour is the supreme law means to say that all other laws cannot or should not contradict the great law, that they are derivative from the Great Law, that they are valid only to the degree that they express the Great Law, and that, if they be preferred to the Great Law or lead one to break the Great Law, this particular law is not obliging; no concrete law can contradict the Great Law, but only be a particularizing or concretization of the Great Law. If there is conflict between laws, the Great Law takes precedence and nullifies the conflicting law.

Once Jesus' audience gets this far with him in the parable, it might begin to feel uneasy. The priest and Levite seemed to act in a holy way, but, since the man is only half-dead, is what they did the will of God, as revealed to Moses?

The motivation of the Samaritan

If the priest and Levite are moved by their sense of obedience to Moses, the Samaritan is moved by compassion. This compassion seems to create a different reaction to the fallen Jew, but the Samaritan, a believer in Yahweh as his history claims, only seems to react differently. That is, he too is keeping the Law of Moses, not disobeying it. His compassion is a sign which indicates what law to follow that will please God. The priest and Levite chose one of the Mosaic laws as determinative here; the Samaritan chose another to follow. That he chose the law of love of neighbour suggests that compassion is a good guide to what God wants. If the priest and Levite felt compassion (may we not presume they did?), they did not interpret their sense of compassion as a sign of what law to follow.

The actions of the Samaritan

Under the impulse of compassion and following the will of God which compassion expresses, the Samaritan is given a series of actions which, ironically, take up more literary space than do the descriptions of the priest and Levite taken together. From wine and oil (cleansing and healing elements in the time of Jesus), to walking beside his mule to let the injured man ride, to the offer of as much money as his care might cost — the activity of the Samaritan is thorough. His love for his neighbour has been translated into costly actions. How different is his analysis and reaction to the situation than were those of the priest and Levite!

The lessons of the Parable

The lesson of the parable is in fact two-fold; Jesus wants it so, as his chosen words indicate.

1. On the one hand, the audience must admit that, though the conduct of the priest and the Levite seems praiseworthy, the life-saving actions of the Samaritan are truly according to the mind of God, are what God would have done, for there is only one great Commandment, God says: love of God and love of neighbor. Thus, the Samaritan has performed those actions by which one can inherit the kingdom of God. Here we should recall what question opened up the debate between Jesus and the lawyer: "Doing what will I inherit the Kingdom of God?" The Samaritan has shown precisely the kind of 'doing' which God expects from those who expect to enter into His Kingdom.

2. On the other hand, greatest of ironies: it is the Samaritan, the enemy, and not the compatriots of the fallen Jew, who saves the Jew. It is the enemy who loves the enemy. And so one realizes what the answer to the lawyer's second question "If I am to love my neighbour as I love myself, who is my neighbour?" must be: My neighbour is anyone in need.

We should understand that in the Jewish circles of Jesus' time, many pious people sought to interpret the neighbour in the phrase "love your neighbour as yourself". There would be no disagreement about loving a pious Jew. There would be some disagreement about whether one should love a sinful Jew — perhaps the argument would more properly center in "what actions should I perform in favour of a sinner?" Certainly, Jesus' way of associating with sinners was vigorously criticized by many pious people. But what about those who were not Jewish, for instance those gentiles who dedicated themselves to Yahweh, and practiced His Law? Does the great commandment apply to them, too? There was great debate here, in part because many thought that the Law applied to physical descendants of Abraham only. But to identify one's neighbour simply by the description, 'one in need', without concern whether or not the person is Jewish, pious, convert — this is hard to swallow.

Jesus' teaching through this parable means to clarify both who is my neighbour and doing what will I inherit the Kingdom of God. Certainly, he means to teach that the neighbour is anyone in need. But he ends his discussion with the lawyer by saying, 'You see what the Samaritan did? Do likewise, to anyone in need. This is the way to inherit the Kingdom of God'. Jesus suggests that compassion helps identify the will of God. True compassion will not contradict God's law, but only help lead one to practice it.

Further comment on the circumstances leading to the parable

The specialist had opened a discussion with the question, "What must I do to inherit eternal life?" That he is identified as specialist in the Law means that the discussion to follow is on the level of professional interpretation of the Law. Sensing the challenge to his own claim to know the Law, Jesus puts the question back on the specialist, "What do you say?" Surprisingly, the lawyer answers, giving what was understood by most everyone to be the beginnings of the laws which one must 'do', i.e. obey, in order to inherit eternal life. That he answers his own question is indeed surprising, since he spoke up in public to learn what Jesus' opinion was. Jesus can only second the specialist's statement, and so he brings the discussion to a close: we now know that Jesus and the specialist both teach that to inherit eternal life, we must 'do' the Law.

But the discussion is not finished, in fact; at least the lawyer is not finished. Luke says that 'he puts Jesus to the test' — as though he had not put him to the test with his first question? The lawyer wants Jesus to commit himself as to who is the 'neighbor' we are to love.

Now, the specialist offers no answer to his question, as he did earlier; Jesus is to speak and be judged.

The answer Jesus gives is his parable and the conclusion he draws from it in question form. First, the parable clearly shows who should be loved: anyone in need; here is the object of love. But again who 'did' the loving? Who 'did' what is recognized as necessary be done to inherit eternal life? With his remarks, brought about by the lawyer's second question, Jesus not only teaches who is to be loved, i.e. who is my 'neighbor', but makes clear, by the same parable, what one must 'do' to inherit eternal life — and so in this way he gives his answer to the original question. Jesus has proposed a fictitious story by which he can answer two questions at the same time, each of which is concerned with the meaning of neighbor, each of which is concerned with doing what is necessary to inherit eternal life.

Is there an end to this story, in which we find the parable? On the one hand, Jesus does answer the questions put to him; in that sense, there is an end to the debate with the lawyer. On the other hand, what finally did the lawyer and the rest of Jesus' audience think and decide? To that question the story is left open. Jesus teaches; it is up to others to learn.

3. THE FOOLISH RICH MAN (LUKE 12, 16-20 [15-21])

Our parable consists of vv. 16-20; it is embedded in a story, Luke 12, 15-21 which has three teachings; after considering Luke's first teaching (vv. 13-14) and then attending to the second teaching which begins with v. 15, we will identify the third and final lesson, v. 21.

The parable itself runs from v. 16 ("*The land of a rich man was enormously productive...*") through v. 20 ("*You fool! This very night your life will be demanded from you; and then who will get what you have gathered for yourself?*"). Luke thinks that his reader will best understand the parable through both the introduction to it, v. 15, and Jesus' conclusion to it, v. 21. Both the introduction and the conclusion contain words of Jesus, with the introductory v. 15 warning against "seeking ever more goods" and the final v. 21 directing one's thoughts to "being rich before God". But the entire episode, i.e. introduction, parable and conclusion — occurs as the result of a dialogue about money, vv. 13-14. These two verses, the first teaching, are worth a moment's attention, since Luke has tied them to the verses we are interested in.

Remote context (v.v. 14-15)

True to the style of Gospel writing, we meet in v. 13 a man who is, as we say, 'faceless'; all we know about him (or are allowed to know about him) is material essential to the point the Evangelist wants to make. Thus, negatively, we do not know his name, his looks, his age, where he comes from — and finally what happened to him after this moment, even whether or not he got his share of the inheritance from his brother. What we do know is what is essential to Luke's point: there is an inheritance involved, the speaker has a brother who seems unwilling to share this inheritance, and apparently the brother (probably the elder brother) has such a hold on the inheritance that the man before Jesus has no recourse but to seek help from a judge; too, this man is willing to make his case public. Most of all, the man wants money (or possessions). The upshot of this very particular description of the man is to call attention to one thing: there is a question here of wanting money. There is no sign that either brother is poor or in need: there is just the desire for money. The desire for money/possessions is not called evil: it is the lead-in to our parable.

The man's cry to Jesus (v. 13) is a plea that Jesus pass judgment, act as judge. We remember that it was a common enough first-century AD practice that a person, who encountered a holy man or a legal specialist (e.g. a Scribe or Rabbi), could ask him, even on the street, to pass judgment on a legal issue; the formal courts were not the only way to resolve a legal problem, especially the non-criminal ones. Jesus refuses to be the judge in this matter. True to his calling, Jesus pursues another direction, which is that of teaching — a teaching which serves to announce the Kingdom of God, especially the call to repentance for sin; Jesus concerns himself with nothing else but this. This, a reminder of what he is about, is his first teaching.

Immediate context (v. 15)

After his remark to the man seeking his intervention, Jesus turns to the crowd that is around him at this moment. He teaches, issuing a warning and explaining briefly why his warning is reasonable.

The warning is that one is to avoid 'greed'. (Note that Jesus does not call either brother greedy; the request for a judicial decision is simply used by Jesus as the basis for a teaching he wants to give; often Jesus will take advantage of a question or remark to teach what he thinks important.)

We must immediately make a distinction about greed. On the one hand, greediness is an evil in itself; the unending desire to accumulate just for the sake of accumulating is an aberration of proper, moral conduct and is to be avoided always. On the other hand, greediness can be seen as a quality which is driven by the desire to live;

in this sense, a human being, which by definition must depend for existence and life on something (or Someone) other than himself, must set about accumulating all that can assure him of life — this can be an unending and anxious search for this 'all'. Though one presumes that Jesus preaches against greed (amassing money for its own sake) in the first sense, it is the second sense (total dependence for one's longevity) that moves him here to condemn greed.

The teaching gives the reason for keeping oneself from being greedy: 'life does not come from increasing one's possessions'. Now one will not disagree with the reason Jesus gives to justify his warning: while goods do contribute to survival and quality of life, in a very essential way survival and quality of life does not depend simply on more and more goods. Strictly speaking, God is the one who decides who will live and in what condition one will live. Again, there is no teaching here that a human being's life and quality of life does not depend on goods; Jesus means to point out the essential cause of life and quality of life: God. Wealth can never take over the role reserved for God, when one seeks to have life and have a good life. (Note that the words of the foolish man speak of both long life and quality of life; ultimately, the teaching of Jesus concerns 'long life'.)

Jesus now offers a parable or fictitious story which he thinks will demonstrate in a more picturesque, literary way why riches cannot, in the ultimate sense, give life. One can err; one can be a fool in this matter, unless one understands the truth about the source of life. Put another way, one must be able to distinguish between the essential source of life (and death) and the secondary cause of life (and death). To put one's trust in the secondary cause and thereby ignore or deny the reality of the essential source of life, is to be, as the parable says, a fool. It is this false belief that creates greediness, i.e. the constant desire to have more and more of what, I think erroneously, will by itself assure me life; it will also create anxiety, the quality which dogs a man to worry about securing a life which he defines as totally dependent on 'having things'.

Jesus' position in this matter, a position gathered from the general teaching of Jesus, is that our dependence for life is dependence on our Father; such dependence, such a relationship based on mutual love, cannot produce anxiety. There is, in Jesus' view, no love for us from money, and so there is not the assurance from money that is like the assurance I have from God's love for me.

The story of the rich man

If one reads the parable alone, without reference to its introduction (v. 15) or to its conclusion (v. 21), one finds it somewhat difficult to detect anything foolish in the rich man's thinking. After all, all the parable says is that this man had an unexpectedly rich crop and saw in it the chance to have a nice life and to be secure for a long time. What is wrong with that?

The interpretation of the parable we divide into three parts. That the first part has to do with greed and wealth might be confusing at first sight, for greed is not always about money, and money is not always the object of greed. Too, greed is in all cases wrong; money can be a good thing. We treat them together here because of Jesus' two introductory words — one about greed, the other about life not depending on wealth; here he intertwines greed and wealth and we follow suit.

A. *First interpretation — the parable in the light of Jesus' introduction: greed and wealth*

It is our being under the influence of Jesus' introduction to the parable that we suspect that the man is thinking wrongly. It is verse 15, and not the parable in and of itself, which points up that we are truly in the presence of erroneous thinking. As always, introduction to a parable gives guidance to identify the lesson of the parable.

Put another way, we can recognize a good meaning to the man's "many good things which assure life for many years". But we can also suspect that this phrase means that the man fully expects to live for many years precisely because, in his judgment, his wealth is the only thing essential for living many years. The second option is possible, but it becomes certain, given that the story is told about greed (v. 15), the result of which is thought to be source of life.

Finally, what surely makes the second option certain is the sudden, unexpected word of God (v. 20). This word reveals the relativity of wealth as regards continued living. Beyond wealth, and its life-giving qualities, is another Power and Authority, which, no matter what wealth has to offer, can make a quick and sudden end to life and so to the value of wealth. It is God's will that decides life and death, and wealth is secondary to His will, so is wealth then the only source of life?

To bring into the picture the voice of God and its condemnation (you fool!) is to question Jesus' audience about its relationship with God. Does it know that He and He alone decides life and death? Jesus is not here speaking against possessions, nor against their value for life; he is speaking here about a man who thinks that wealth is what keeps him alive. In a world which admits that God is above all other creatures in power and will, to depend on wealth for one's continuance in life and on God, is to deny the meaning of Yahweh and, to the degree that one gives wealth the power of god, make wealth into God; the secondary source of life takes the place of the primary source of life. Indeed, one should be greedy, if he ignores that God is the ultimate decider how long one lives, how soon one dies. The trust usually acknowledged as owed to God is now given to wealth. To look on wealth as the final cause of the prolongation of life is foolishness.

What a fool, to have put his trust in the wrong thing — and in such a crucial matter as life!

B. *Second interpretation of the parable — from within the parable itself: the reality of death*

1. Clearly the initial verses of the parable mean to set the scene: this man has received a bumper crop and must decide what to do with it; so far, we meet only a fact and a need to make a decision. Then, the man makes his decision, apparently a prudent one since he seems to have found a way to secure his life for many years. Since one is responsible, through work, to preserve one's life, the parable does not criticize the man's gathering his new goods. But suddenly, with the suddenness of unforeseen tragedy, the voice from heaven intervenes to announce the man's 'death tonight'. Here one can see the beginning of Jesus' lesson: the man had not figured the possibility of present death in his decision-making. Here is the parable's point: how foolish not to think, in one's planning for the future, that one might die immediately! Certainly, one must, as a rational being, prepare for the future, but more: one must prepare for any eventuality, including no future. Thus, the man is ultimately a figure who, in ignoring the full range of possibilities and the reality of death at any time, acts like a fool; we remember the warnings about and the prayers for the gift of wisdom that flow throughout the Old Testament. This is the central teaching of the parable: it is foolishness to ignore the reality of death, which happens not when we decide, but when Another decides.

2. The last words of the Voice from Heaven show the effects of foolishness about death: not having taken into account the imminent possibility of death, one has totally worked for someone else — he has no idea who! Neither has he gained anything by his increased wealth, nor does he even know who will enjoy it. He has, equivalently, worked for a 'somebody else' and not for himself — and how foolish that is!

Thus, we have a) heard the teaching of Jesus that life does not come ultimately from possessions, and b) seen why a man who thinks that life does come from possessions is foolish. Jesus' audience can only agree that one is foolish who prepares for the future by putting all one's confidence on money, that he will always have it, and who forgets that finally only God makes one live and die.

Notice that in this second interpretation of the parable, it is not precisely greed and its limitations which is the subject, but the stupidity of making this, or any decision without averting at all as to who controls life and death, without admitting that there is One who can act whenever He wishes, sooner or later, with no concern for what wealth I may possess.

C. *Third interpretation of the parable — under the influence of v. 21: a proper use of wealth*

Thus far, Jesus has warned about greediness (that is driven by the belief that life depends essentially on possessions) and about a failure to know the reality which is the unpredictability of death. Both of these aspects (one beginning with v. 15 and the other presented in v. 20) of the second lesson are in a sense negative: they show wrong attitudes, both of which can be called foolishness. What we need is a positive teaching, or at least the opening to such a teaching; in other words, I know what the man should not have done — what should he have done?

At v. 21 Jesus now looks back at the story he has just told, at the man who acted so foolishly. He reveals in his analysis of the man's story that the man's thinking not only showed no consideration for the possibility of 'death tonight' and the subsequent foolishness of handing over all his goods to an unknown 'other', but also that he has not made provision for treasure in heaven.

In what consists 'treasure in heaven' of which the man has none? One might suggest various things that make up heavenly treasure, but the definition of heavenly treasure is not the concern here. What is of concern, as is clear from Luke's presentation in the Gospel and Acts, that a central means to having the 'treasure in heaven' is making sure, by using one's possessions properly, that there is no one in need. The Gospel and Acts serve as the dictionary in which we learn what makes up this aspect of one's treasure in heaven. There are various ways in which one uses wealth: some are asked to leave all to follow Jesus, many are asked to use their wealth in support of 'the poor, the crippled, the blind and the lame'. Peter and others are good examples of the former. The Good Samaritan, Zacchaeus (19, 1-10) and Barnabas (Acts, 4, 36-37) are examples of the latter. We also are given a sad story about the ruler who, after being invited to leave all and follow Jesus, preferred to keep his wealth and so would not follow Jesus.

The parable's central figure never even thinks for a moment of anyone but himself. This is not to say that I can know this solely from the man's words to himself; I need Jesus' interpretation of the man's words to understand the full meaning of his thinking. But, once I understand his thinking, I finally understand the complete teaching of Jesus through this parable: one must provide treasure in heaven or else one has nothing there — a key way to have treasure in heaven is to help those in need, to use the bumper crop to gain treasure in heaven, rather than to ignore the possible nearness of death and the futility of greed. And one understands better how the opening concern of the story, 'inheritance' or wealth, leads Jesus to think of the proper use of wealth as a key to having treasure in heaven. This kind of wealth, making sure that no one is in need — the effect of this will not be left behind after death, but will assure enjoyment of the 'treasure in heaven'.

Conclusion

We have seen that the parable of Jesus about a rich man, who gains unexpectedly, only to lose everything through sudden death, is a particularized response from Jesus to the person who 'wanted a share of his father's inheritance' and the rest of his audience. At first, Jesus affirms that he is not a judge in these matters, and thus reaffirms his conviction that he is to call for repentance of sins. Second, he warns against the deep-seated opinion that says that life is preserved and developed by wealth alone. To be greedy for wealth on the supposition that it will provide a long life is foolishness. The man of the parable is an example of this: his confidence in wealth meant little, for by it he did not save his life. Then, the parable gives its warning: one cannot look to wealth and its use without looking to God, that only by understanding the place of God in one's life and death can one begin to think rightly about the power and limitation of wealth.

It is logical to conclude that to ignore God and put one's confidence in wealth is the height of foolishness; the signal example: just consider how sudden and unplanned-for death shows death to be powerless before it. Too, such an attitude toward death, which is a true master of the human being, ends by ironically giving all one's wealth to someone to whom one never intended it. Finally, guided by v. 21, we learn further how to understand the foolishness of the rich man: he had wealth alright, but never using it rightly, e.g. making sure that no one was in need, he showed he had no treasure in heaven — and so when he went to heaven? He had…nothing!

Immediately following vv. 13-21 is a discourse of Jesus which counsels against an anxiety about preserving life that excludes the truth that our Father, God who can do anything and wants to love us, will take care of us; in this view, we are to trust Him who loves us, and seek to love Him in return. Anxiety occurs when one depends, not on a loving Giver, but upon unloving wealth. Anxiety cannot be the Christian's; it is a denial of the role of God our Father in our life. If there must be anxiety in one's life, let it be the anxiety to love God and neighbor, so as to have life and riches forever. In its own way this discourse underlines the need to know the truth about life, that God is essential to it and that longing to gain the Kingdom of God is man's highest priority. To know the truth about life is true wisdom, the wisdom which assuredly leads to happiness. One can look upon this subsequent discourse of Jesus (12, 22-34) as the full teaching of Jesus begun in the story which contains our parable.

A Consideration about Wisdom

A brief explanation of the term 'wisdom' can help us better appreciate Jesus' concern about it here; 'wisdom' concerned his audience, too. Wisdom, or knowledge in the ancient world, that is the world before Jesus, was a means which served a purpose. (In its original sense, 'philosophy' was the love of wisdom, which love demands a search for the most loveable wisdom.) Knowledge was considered a primary and necessary means to happiness. Happiness is the goal, knowledge is a key means to it; indeed, the rationality of man, that man has a mind, clearly argues to this. Thus, in this way of thinking, one does not speculate or learn or study or do research just for the pure joy of learning. One does these things because by doing them one has a better and better chance of being happy.

In the use of the mind to achieve happiness, it was believed, there really is no limit to subject matter: the wise man in search of wisdom considers such subjects as 'the heavens, the earth and under the earth' and all that is in them, e.g. the matter which is the concern of physics and chemistry, of political science and personal psychology, the gods, all the living and non-living creatures, the demon world, economics and art, the lives of the great and the small, virtue and moral codes — everything. In particular, the conviction is that the more one knows, the more one can predict the future, thereby assuring oneself of happiness, for an unpredictable future is the potential opening to failure and unhappiness. Kings surrounded themselves with Wise Men (sometimes called Magi), and were particularly interested in such anxious questions about the future as: should I lead my kingdom into war? If one can only know enough, runs the belief, he can secure his happiness.

In Israel's case, there are, at first glance at the Old Testament, two means to happiness, a) obedience to the will of God and b) knowledge, i.e. wisdom.

A. As is clear throughout the first books of the Old Testament, Israel conceived of God as a King who made a covenant with 'His People'. This covenant meant to assure Israel of the King's good will and power, and to assure to God the obedience of His People. God would provide all that was necessary for the happiness of Israel; if one were to ask how one might be happy, the answer from these early books is: obey God, for He knows what is best for us.

B. Later in Israel's history, when the People had come under the forceful influence of pagan countries (like Assyria, Babylonia, Persia and Greece), what was a hallmark of those peoples — namely a human search for a wisdom that controls and thus assures happiness — was so attractive that such wisdom became a characteristic of Israel. It was a wisdom that was rooted in man's ability to think, learn and assimilate — through human reason alone (as regards morality, we call this 'ethics'). Traditionally, then, Israel had sought happiness by obedience with absolute trust in Yahweh, its Father and Groom. Now, under foreign influences, one is invited to act because of one's study that culminates in one's own rational conviction that, "as I see it" (based on human, thorough study), this or that is the best to do be happy.

Israel is faced now with two ways to find happiness: the old way, one is obedience to God, and the new way, one trusts in one's own analysis and reasoning. Put another way, one does such-and-such, no longer because God commands it, but because from my study I conclude that it is reasonable. Clearly, there was danger in reliance or dependence simply on one's own reasoning powers, even on the wisdom of the wisest of human beings; the proliferation of philosophies and theologies and moralities in the ancient world, and dissatisfaction with all of them, witness to that.

In the long run, what Israel did was to offer this solution: the commands of God are the truest wisdom; if human reason is a trustworthy tool to achieve happiness, we must begin to consider God's reasoning powers, used on our behalf, to be the most absolutely trustworthy tool to achieve our happiness. With this thought, one begins to look at the commands of God, not simply as trustworthy commands of a Superior, but as the most reasonable way to live life and be happy. It falls to us to think not simply of authority and obedience, of master and servant, but to study to understand why the command of God is the most reasonable way to do things, to live life and thereby give human reason its proper function and respect. If I do not always understand the commands of God? Even so, Israel's final position is the conviction that His commands, His ways, though far from my ways, are true wisdom. In this manner, Israel made a marriage of obedience and thinking: the best I can know for my happiness is the command of God. Thus, Israel always wants to know what God wants, but also always tries to understand it, to see how rational His command is. In this regard, the man of the parable relied solely on his own assessment of his future, which proved very limited and ultimately destructive. He did not take into consideration God's wisdom in these matters. It is the glory of man that he makes his own wisdom the wisdom of God.

4. UPON THE RETURN OF THE MASTER (LUKE 12, 35-48) — INDEED, THREE PARABLES

Context

In Luke 12, 35-48 we have three parables: the actions of servants and master on the occasion of a wedding (35-38), the vigilance of a master against thieves (39-40) and the answer (42-48) to Peter's question, "Lord, is this parable addressed (only) to us or to everyone?" (41). The response to Peter follows directly upon the second of our three parables, that dealing with protection against robbers, but the word might include the first fictitious story as well.

Jesus had already devoted some time to describing what should be our understanding of death's place in life (cf. the biting contrast between 12, 19 ['I now live a long life'] and 20 ['Tonight you die']) and of God the Father's care of His children and treasure in heaven; these thoughts lead to consider the reality that we here on earth should be preparing ourselves for our life in God's heavenly kingdom. It is the thought of the end of life that now governs vv. 35-48, which are played out in our three parables. Jesus' concern about our entrance into the eternal divine kingdom focuses upon both the alertness needed for 'the call at any time' and the kind of life which is guided by the thought of having to always be ready for the call to that Kingdom. The rich man earlier had no thought about when he might die or about having treasure in Heaven. In our three present parables Jesus once again teaches about this readiness to die and the life one lives in anticipation of that call.

The first parable, vv. 35-38

A. *Verses 35-36*

We have before us an image of a household master or lord about to return from celebrations at a wedding. The uncertainty of the time of his return home accurately reflects customs in Palestine — even today, who knows exactly when he will return from a great banquet? Upon the master's return, at whatever hour of the night, the servants will have things to do, things that call for the master's approval before he finally goes to bed; they must be ready.

In this all-too-frequent scenario the servants are to keep themselves ready, ready to fulfil all the duties which precede the sleep of the master; indeed, they wait for any instructions he may give them upon his return from the wedding. To be prepared for whatever the master may require, the servants are dressed properly: i.e. they are dressed in their clothes suitable to their work and have candles or lanterns in their hands. They are ready for the expected coming of the master. Their waiting is their duty, a duty always kept uppermost in their minds. No other thing should weaken this readiness, should stand in the way of a smooth return of the master into his home. Indeed it often was the case that servants used their lamps to light the final path which leads the master to his property and door. Yes, one might think it is easy enough and perhaps defensible that this or that servant fall asleep in waiting for the delayed master; it is natural that the lamp of this or that servant becomes useless as it burns out in the wait for the master. Yet, it is ultimately, finally unpardonable that any servant fail to keep himself fully ready for the return of the master. Whatever serves that readiness must be done, for there is nothing more important than to be ready for the master. And no one in Jesus' audience would disagree with his description of the first-century relationship between master and servant, a relationship which makes this attentiveness an absolute priority.

B. *Verses 37-38*

These verses are notable in three ways. First, the accent is on a happy conclusion to the story: "Happy are they…" There is always present the note of possible failure, but it is not mentioned and apparently not of concern here. Rather, Jesus concentrates on the joy that follows upon readiness to greet the master. Second, the story loses its touch with custom, indeed Palestinian reality, when Jesus notes that the master (at no matter what the hour of his arrival may be) will put on serving clothes and serve his servants. Such a gesture, in human terms, seems most unlikely. Jesus must have been thinking of another 'homecoming', that of the faithful disciples entering into the presence of their Master, Jesus. Apparently here Jesus means to underline the precious value of readiness "to serve with lamps lit", for the reward of readiness is wonderful. Finally, Jesus underlines the demands of readiness: no matter what the hour or how long the wait, if one is ready, happiness will be the result when the master comes. And the master's return often is late: the 'second or the third hour'.

In ancient times in Israel, the twenty-four hours that made up the day were divided into two equal, twelve-hour halves. The night's twelve hours lasted from 6:00 pm till 6:00 am. This 12-hour period was further divided into three 'hours', the first, the second and the third 'hour'. Jesus refers to the second or third hours of the night, thus between10:00 pm and 2:00 am or between 2:00 am and 6:00 am. (Romans divided the 12-hour night into four hours or watches).

(Another aspect of the time of the Master's coming: one recalls the tension in the Gospels between the apparent expectation that Jesus would return very soon for Judgment and the growing sense of a lack of knowledge about when he might come. However one explains the late coming of the Lord, it is clear that, for Luke, there is no point anymore in trying to predict the time He will come.)

The second parable (vv. 39-40)

Jesus had asked his hearers to imagine themselves as the servants who wait for the return of their master; with this picture he urges them to readiness, a readiness which will bring great joy. Now, in a second image, he asks them to liken themselves, not to servants, but to a master. Again, the subject, readiness for an imminent coming, remains the same. The coming is that of a thief — an unlikely description of God, but it is God's coming he has in mind. As Jesus opens this parable, he calls for the participation of the listeners; the proposition he offers them depends on logic, human reasoning ("You know..."). So often Jesus depends on this form of teaching in his parables. Certainly, he is capable of commands to act in such-and-such a moral way, but also he often appeals to the hearer's judgment — "I won't tell you what to do; you be the judge in this matter!"

One can only answer 'yes, the owner of a house would certainly protect his possessions against a thief', especially if he knew when the thief was coming. Jesus reminds his audience that the Judgment Day is coming, something well worth being prepared for. His audience does not, however, know when that will be; should they be any the less ready, and should they be always ready lest they fail the Judgment when it comes? Here, this parable coincides in meaning with the first parable of servants awaiting the master whenever he comes — always be ready!

The image Jesus uses of himself, the Son of Man, seems to have its first reference to a figure used in Daniel 7, where the book of Judgment, at first in the hands of God, is given to "One like a son of man" — this, signifying that now this Son of Man will exercise the divine role of Judge of the world. This title, Son of Man, appears in other contexts to describe Jesus, contexts which have no immediate reference to final Judgment; this is a sign of the development of the image to reflect the many other divine powers and tasks God shares with Jesus. Unexpectedly perhaps is the fact that only one time does this title appear elsewhere than in the Gospels, namely in Stephen's vision in Acts 7 (perhaps a development out of the contemporaneous theology that saw Michael the Archangel as the One like a son of man who stands before God). Interestingly, no one else but Jesus calls Jesus 'Son of Man'. Notably, when Jesus speaks about his death-glorification, he prefers to use the title of Son of Man, that figure who will, after suffering, return from the glorious right hand of his Father to be Judge the world.

The first two parables, then, urge readiness for the Judgment. They explicitly underline the joy of one who is ready no matter when the Lord comes. Certainly, the picture is of the end, of the Judgment, but the first two parables mean to stress not threat but blessedness for the one who is ready, for the one who can pass the judgment. Elsewhere Jesus has talked about the hindrances to entering into the Kingdom of God; now he stresses the joy of being ready to enter that Kingdom.

The third parable (vv. 42-48)

After Jesus finishes with the second parable, Peter speaks up, "Lord, is it with us in mind only that you speak this parable or is it with a view to everyone?" Jesus, as he so often does, will not answer a question directly, but takes advantage of the question to give the teaching which he thinks is valuable for his questioner. Thus, Jesus does not choose from the alternatives Peter offers or follow Peter's distinction between 'them' and 'us'. Rather, he emphasizes again his teaching about readiness for the return of a master, a teaching which we can assume is meant for 'all', Peter and 'them' — yet, there will be something distinctive for Peter, for 'us', which soon will be addressed in the parable.

Jesus talks again about readiness, building on the first two parables concerned with preparedness. First, Jesus repeats his positive encouragement to faithful service: blessed, happy will the servant be; his reward for fidelity to the master will be vigorously rewarded. Then, he adds his two new elements. These have to do with servants who fail to be ready — their difference here is that one fails, while knowing very well the commands and expectations of his master; the other fails, though he knows very little of the commands and expectations of his master.

A. *The unprepared servant*

Readiness, if the term is not already clear to the audience, means that one never forgets about the return of the master, no matter how delayed it may be, that one continues faithfully in one's assigned tasks while awaiting the return of the master. But in this third parable, Jesus spends much time in describing the world of the unjust servant, one who ignores or lets himself forget the coming of his master, and lives in such a way that, when the master does come, the master will be very displeased. Jesus' audience knew about these types of servants, too.

Here, in this third parable, there is the twin emphasis on both awareness of the return of the Master and of the Judgment that comes with his return. On the one hand, Jesus urges all his hearers to be always alert for God's coming, that one lives in the perpetual awareness of this coming. Thus, one never forgets that 'He is coming'. On the other hand, never to forget that He is coming means He is coming to judge, and so one's alertness to his coming includes a person's never forgetting to do the deeds on which one will be judged. Thus one always is mindful not just of His coming, but of His judgment of one's moral life: one must pass the Judgment to be rewarded for faithfulness. It suggests, second, that a loss of awareness of the coming and of the consequent judgment is a reason which leads one to ignore the wishes of the master: woe to him, then, who not only forgets about the master, but allows himself to perform deeds that are contrary to what the master expects. It seems that this parable points up the fact that injustices on earth can make one forget, can dull one to the Final Coming. To forget the twin realities of the coming of the Lord and of His Judgment can lead to living a life which will someday be punished when the Master comes; vice-versa, living a punishable life makes one lose one's awareness of the Final Judgement.

B. *The one to whom much has been given and the one to whom little has been given*

Jesus introduces the subject of the 'difference in remissful servants'. These are servants who have little or no 'knowledge of God's commands'; their degree of knowledge, or lack thereof, leads to greater or lesser punishment for these servants who ignore the coming of God. The one who knows the will of God, but fails to do it — he will receive severe punishment. Conversely, the one who does not know the will of God and so fails to do it — he will receive a lesser punishment. One can understand the words of Jesus without reference to context — i.e. sinning in ignorance is less punishable than sinning in full knowledge of right and wrong. But what do they mean in context?

What scholars ask is precisely whether or not these two kinds of servants — one who knows, and one who does not — reflects a situation which Jesus' disciples either face right now, or will soon face. Is it possible that Jesus is drawing the traditional distinction between Israel, who knows the will of God in the Law of Moses, and the Gentiles, who are described as being without light? Or, is it possible that Jesus is speaking about the wise of Israel who know the Law and the crowds of Israel who know little of it? But perhaps Jesus is not speaking about his generation at all, but rather about future disciples of the next generations who become specialists, as it were, in knowing the will of God, as opposed to future disciples who have little specialist knowledge of the divine will? Is Jesus pointing to a division in the Christian community expected some day in the future, which will have in it those who study and know very profoundly the will of God and have in it, too, those who pass through Christian life with just a rudimentary knowledge of the will of God? Putting it more baldly, does he expect such a division in the Christian community between leaders and followers, on the basis of knowledge of God's will? Is he talking about future disciples in roles of leadership which demands special or professional knowledge, and about future disciples who will be the 'flock' entrusted to these leaders, a flock which has no professional knowledge about the profundity of their faith (nor the gifts of the Spirit, described by Paul in 1 Cor 12, or by Luke in Acts 13, 1-3), but depend for this on their leaders or shepherds?

And this series of musings leads to the conclusion that, whatever context Jesus had in mind when he gave this parable (his own generation or world, the time of the Church, and then of Luke himself), people recalled Jesus' parable precisely to counter tendencies which existed in their own times, among their own sad experiences. More directly, did Luke in his own readership in Rome know of servants who did understand the will of God and yet failed to live according to what they knew, and of others who did not know the will of God and failed? Is this parable included in Luke's Gospel, precisely because he knew his community needed to hear it? If so, the wise will be punished for their disobedience more severely than will be the ignorant.

While a number of scholars think that this third parable reflects the punishments to be given to leaders and followers in the church, there is one serious flaw in this suggestion. If one looks carefully at the parable, he finds no distinction between 'him who knows a lot' and 'him who know little'. The proper distinction is between 'him who knows' and 'him who does not know'. In looking for suitable parallel in real life, one thinks of the believer, who knows the commands of Jesus, and the Gentile or pagan, who knows not the will and teachings of Jesus. If this be the right approach, we have here, not a description of different situations within the church, but of the difference between one in the church and one outside it.

Following this train of thought Jesus offers another. It speaks now not to simple alertness to the coming of God, but to the reward or punishment for conduct which is conditioned by knowledge and lack thereof. It speaks to the fact that from one who is given much, much will be expected. This saying focuses the end of Jesus' parables not on those who have no knowledge of God's will, but on those who are versed in what God wants and expects, but disobey. The lesson here can be verified in non-religious areas of life and not only in one's life with God. How often the person who abuses a gift ends up with no gift at all!

And it is with this last statement from Jesus that we see more clearly how this third, extended parable answers Peter's supposition, while allowing Jesus to address all who serve God. Peter wanted to know if fidelity to one's tasks, which depend on a constant alertness to God's Final Coming, is a fidelity of such a person as Peter and the other Twelve or a fidelity that pertains to many, many others. It is clear now that, on the one hand, everyone is called to constant readiness and to its rewards, but in the Final Judgment, one can understand how much more can be expected from him who knows Jesus and his teachings, how much less can be expected from him who knows nothing of God's commands. And if the scholars' opinion cited above is accurate? Given that Luke's audience had structures of authority, such as administrator, prophet, teacher, but included many others who had no gift of the Spirit, Luke at the end speaks strongly to the Christian leadership — through the encouraging and threatening words of Jesus.

5. THE BARREN FIG TREE (LUKE 13, 4-9)

The story

All Palestinian Jews could understand the agricultural elements of this parable about the barren fig tree; many Jews, even with small plots of land, had vineyards in which one could also find a fig tree. The fig tree, which grows to a height of some 30 to 40 feet, lives even on rocky soil, a soil for many vineyards in Palestine. The fig tree was ever appreciated, not only for its delicious fruit (especially the earliest mature figs), but also for its large leaves which produced a much appreciated shade for those beneath it. Our story, however, suggests that we have here a vineyard which is more than a "small plot of land": we read of an owner who does nothing in the vineyard but visit it, leaving the oversight to a vinedresser who has the actual day-to-day responsibility for the owner's garden. In normal circumstances one would expect a fig tree at the earliest to produce fruit in its third year; the first two years are a time of maturation towards fruit production. In short, Jesus has presented his audience with a story that is very true to life.

But the fig tree also has symbolic value. The fig tree was used in texts of the Old Testament as a figure of Israel. Jesus' audience no doubt understood quickly the direction Jesus' parable was to take: in the spirit of the ancient prophets, who also use agricultural elements to teach, the audience, steeped in knowledge of these prophets, was ready for a new address to Israel.

There was at one time a debate among scholars as to what we might call the "effect" of the parable. On the one hand, the story seems to emphasize the negative: there is no fruit when there should be fruit, there is the command to cut down the fig tree, and there is the opinion of the vinedresser that, should it not produce any fruit in the next year, cut it down. But on the other hand, there is the cautiously positive, the possibility of success: perhaps with a little more care the vineyard will produce its fruit; let us hope. Perhaps we should not think that the one theme excludes the other, but accept the tension indicated in this situation. Indeed, we do not know what the decision was that the vinedresser left to the owner to make — did he think it too late, or did he give the tree another chance? And with another chance, did fruit grow?

The context

Why would Luke recount this simple parable at this precise juncture of his Gospel? The reason for the parable's placement here, in this context, helps us understand better the fullest intention of Jesus. Let us look at what preceded this parable as a way of understanding it.

The preceding story (vv. 1-5)

The story which precedes our parable is its best introduction. The story offers few details, only those necessary to let Jesus make his point. Luke begins: 'At the 'same time' certain people come to Jesus with some news'. The term 'same time' links this story with the immediately preceding urging from Jesus (vv. 54-59) that everyone try to recognize, discern and make sense of the meaning of his being with them, of this 'time' in which the Kingdom of God is being announced and repentance for sins is being called for, the 'time' when one gets one's moral affairs in order before he is brought before the Judge — after which there is no chance of repentance. Looming strongly in Jesus' present messages is need for preparation to enter the Kingdom through repentance; mysteriously, "The Kingdom is among you!" and you must accept what is now here and prepare for its fullness.

The news is brought to Jesus about fellow Galileans. Word is that Pontius Pilate, administrator of Judaea on behalf of Rome, has mixed blood of Galileans with their sacrifices (in the Jerusalem

Temple), an act which makes horrendous an already criminal, wanton abuse of human power and authority toward what the audience knows to be the people God loves. (We have no details about this act of Pilate, but it seems to agree with a general insensitivity and harshness reported about him by historians of the time.)

What these people who bring this message hope to achieve by telling their story to Jesus is not said. There could be a number of expectations on these people's minds. Jesus does have a response to their news.

As one comes to expect, Jesus in the Gospel will make what he will of any comments or questions offered to him. Here he asks back, perhaps unexpectedly, as to what the audience thinks is the lesson from this brutal end of these Galileans: is it that they suffer this unspeakable outrage because these unfortunates are greater sinners than other Galileans (e.g. the Galileans who brought this story) to whom this has not happened? That this disgrace means God is especially displeased with them? Jesus' world is a society that has come to measure guilt by tragedy. The greater the tragedy, the greater the guilt. Indeed the sacred writings of Israel often associate terrible suffering with terrible sin. Jesus' question asks the audience if it judges now that this tragedy reveals that the abused are greater sinners than those who have not suffered such a tragedy. Do you think you are less the sinner because you have not suffered as they have? Because nothing like this has been done to you, do not think of yourselves as the lesser sinners?

Jesus leaves it to his listeners to answer his question. But he assures them of a personal lesson: without repentance, the audience will in some way perish as have these poor Galileans. Implied in Jesus' remark is his conviction that sin will be punished, whether one sees an immediate punishment for sin or not. The norm, he implies, to determine who is the greatest sinner is not external tragedy in one's life, but a fair and honest evaluation of oneself against the commands of the Mosaic Law. And so, with or without tragedy here, sins will be fully paid for.

But Jesus' ultimate teaching is not the statement that one cannot gauge the presence of sin by tragedy. His ultimate teaching is more, much more promising: you will avoid the punishment for sin if only you repent. Jesus may appear somber and threatening here, but in fact he urges avoidance of punishment; he urges here, as through all his life, repentance which allows one to enter nothing less than the very kingdom of Heaven.

In accord with teaching practice, in which repetition is a tool for teaching effectively, Jesus repeats the lesson while making use of another present-day, widely-known tragedy. A tower in the area of Siloam, in the southeast sector of Jerusalem, recently collapsed and killed eighteen people. Again, the question: do you think these deaths were punishment for sins? And do you think that, because no tower has fallen on you, you are not sinners? On the contrary, and Jesus repeats, unless you repent of your sins, you will perish in a way very reminiscent of the deaths of these eighteen people. The final call: in view of impending punishment, please repent!

This teaching of Jesus about repentance follows logically from a major, ever-present theme of the Gospel: acknowledgement of one's sins, repentance for them and readiness to undergo the Final Judgment in order to enter the Kingdom of God. It is true that Jesus defined his public life as an announcement of the kingdom of God (4, 43). But most all of his public life showed the way to entering this kingdom: "I have come (i.e. God has sent me) to call the sinner to repentance" (5, 32).

Conclusion

This teaching of Jesus about the repentance of sinners in vv. 1-5, an exhortation often today in Bibles entitled 'repent or perish', but which really means to encourage repentance, is followed logically by our parable which clearly addresses the imminent punishment of the sinner. The owner of the vineyard finds no fruit on a fig tree and therefore wishes to destroy it. It is clear that in this parable Jesus calls on his listeners' familiarity with the theme of 'God ready to punish Israel because it does not obey the Mosaic covenant, summed up in love of God and love of neighbor'. Jesus has already twice called for repentance in the verses preceding our parable. He represents a period in which God, the owner of the vineyard, has staid His hand and not punished Israel for its disobedience, but uses Jesus to call Israel once more — perhaps, as the parable suggests, for the last time — to produce the good fruit of obedience. Vv. 1-5 did not describe this present situation; they called for repentance, but did not describe God as so close to closing the period for repentance. This element is a particular contribution of our parable.

God is angry and inclined to punish, but now there is a ray of hope. Perhaps if God will wait a while longer before punishing sin, conversion and repentance will take place, good fruit will be produced. Let Jesus, in this picture the vine-dresser, work at it for awhile. Will he stay the hand of God? How long will God wait? We note again what is implicit: the time of Jesus, when he called all to immediate repentance before the end-time, gives way to the time of the disciples in their succeeding generations: how long will God delay His coming, how long will He be patient in his expectation of good fruit?

It is worth noting that, if the figure of the vinedresser is to be understood as Jesus, it is not Jesus who will decide when the tree is no longer worth keeping. In this parable, it seems that God is the one to decide this; Jesus is the one who works at having people repent and is the one who calls on God for patience while Jesus works. That Jesus functions as the intercessor who asks God to be patient — this is not a picture of Jesus we encounter often in the Gospels. For all that, it is a revealing interpretation of Jesus' public life.

6. THE MUSTARD SEED AND THE YEAST (LUKE 13, 18-21) — INDEED, TWO PARABLES

Observations

A. *Two parables together*

It is more likely that these two parables were not said at the same time, though Luke gives the impression they were and so wants his reader to think of them together. Because of this literary strategy, each parable contributes more than it might by itself; i.e. both parables work together to strengthen the same lesson Jesus wants to teach in each of them. It is not uncommon that a writer like Luke would put side by side two elements (and this holds for miracles, too), which were originally separate, so as to make even more vigorous the lesson each parable shares with the other. Oddly enough, Luke finds the parable of the mustard seed as useful as do Matthew and Mark, but neither of the latter decided to recall to their readers the parable of the yeast.

B. *A story preceding the two parables*

The two parables, by themselves, seem to be without reference to what precedes and follows them. But this impression is probably to be doubted, since most often the sequence of materials that Luke employs is chosen consciously by him, as though to say that even the sequence has a lesson to teach. In our case, the parables of mustard seed and yeast follow upon a miracle of healing on the Sabbath and precede the problem put to Jesus, "Will few be saved?" It is to the first combination that our attention is drawn, that between the miracle and the parables.

What leads us in this direction is the small word which introduces the parables, "then". The parables are a sequel ('then'), if not in some sense a conclusion ('therefore') to the story Luke recounts about the cure on the Sabbath. Certainly that story had an ending: with Jesus' defence of his healing, his critics fell silent and the crowds rejoiced over the glorious or splendid things Jesus was doing. But can the parables of mustard seed and yeast also serve as further ending?

C. *Brief analysis of the cure/dispute story (13, 10-17)*

The words of Jesus which the crowd admired so much were meant to explain why Jesus thought he was right to cure a woman who was perpetually bent over, unable to raise herself straight — possessed by a spirit of weakness. (At this time, many physical illnesses were thought to be caused by evil spirits.) When Jesus cures the woman, one can only think that Luke implies that Jesus completely dominates this spirit of weakness; Luke has intentionally presented the major force of evil as one dominated simply by a word of the Lord.

D. *The context*

The cure sets in conflict the president of the local synagogue and Jesus; the conflict is centered on the word 'work', which traditionally in Judaism signifies what should not be done on the Sabbath; curing illness was considered a 'work,' and so forbidden on the Sabbath. In favour of the synagogue president is the reasoning, based on the call to respect the Sabbath: there are six other days for curing, healing — why must you come on the Sabbath when healing is forbidden? Implied is the opinion that the woman could wait one more day and show respect for the Sabbath and then have her cure.

E. *The legal problem of the Sabbath*

The words of Jesus, which are as important for us and Christian tradition as the cure was for the woman, center on two points, one legal and the other theological. First, though the works forbidden on the Sabbath are very numerous, as spelled out by the religious authorities of the time, there can be exceptions made, there can be times when 'work' is allowed on the Sabbath. One is certainly allowed on the Sabbath, Jesus notes, to take an animal to drink water, even though such an action is generally agreed upon as a 'work'. The justification of this exception is rooted in the fact that a man depends on a healthy animal for his own well-being; since God would want the man's well-being, He must want a healthy animal. This exception to the law of the Sabbath in favour of an animal is meant to raise the question: if a man can bring an animal to 'cure its thirstiness' on the Sabbath and thereby save its owner's good health, can I (Jesus) not free or save a human being from the spirit of weakness on the Sabbath and so assure her of good health?

There are particular considerations at issue here which we must stress, though they are not so directly formulated in the story as it is written here. First, the synagogue leader wants the woman to wait one more day in her sickness, but does not ask his animal to wait one more day for a drink. Besides, how should we compare the two subjects, animal and woman? The lesser being, servant of man, is worthy of exception; the other, the human being served by animals, is not? And why does God allow this exception on the Sabbath? It is not the animal which is the major concern of God, but the owner of the animal who will suffer, if his animal suffers. Indeed, God is concerned for everyone in Israel, including this 'daughter of Abraham' (v. 16); every child of Abraham is deserving of the loving kindness promised to Abraham and his descendants. In the light of this divine love, Jesus sees no reason to delay her cure.

Jesus' first point, then, has to do with the reasonableness of an exception to the Sabbath law, especially when one considers that one is on the verge of preferring the well-being of an animal to that of a human being, indeed a daughter of Abraham.

E. *The kingdom of God*

Let us flesh out this last point a bit more. Jesus refers to the woman as a 'daughter of Abraham'; what does this description have to do with her being cured or not. Jesus' audience would know very well the promises made to Abraham and to his offspring. Though there are various elements to these promises, and not all elements are repeated in every reference in every promise made to Abraham, there is a central issue: the children of Abraham are created to worship Him in holiness and justice all the days of their lives, and they will do this, once they are freed from their enemies (cf. the words of Zachary in Luke 1, [73] 74-75). The enemy may be identified as the Romans, or before them the Persians and Greeks, but the enemy is also identified as whatever keeps the Iraelite from full worship of the true God. In this second understanding, the woman, a daughter of Abraham, should have the possibility to worship God in fullness of health, free from her enemy — in this case the spirit of weakness. The cure, then, can be touted as an act of kindness, but we cannot lose sight of the fact that the benefit of cure is the practice of worshipping God as an Israelite can and should. The cure of this woman leads to her glory as full participant her People's worship of God.

It is easy to side with Jesus in his dispute with the synagogue leader: the woman, a daughter of Abraham, deserves love that belongs to one's neighbor and the opportunity to worship God in full union with the rest of the People. But there is even more here than just one cure, or the words to justify it. In the larger picture, we have here a victory of Jesus over an evil spirit. The cure of the woman is one sign, among many, that Jesus has come to give life, or the more complete life. In royal terms, he is, with each cure, beginning to establish the Kingdom of God, a kingdom in which there is no more sickness, no more tears and, indeed, no more death. One might say that whereas others thought of the Kingdom as coming at the end of time, Luke prefers to think of it as beginning now and to be brought to its fullness at the end of time. Consider the defining words of Jesus: "If by the finger of God I drive out demons, then the kingdom of God has come upon you" (11, 20). This explains to some degree why Luke, who knows not when that fullness will come and abandons all attempts to name the time, still feels we are in the 'last times' (cf. Acts 2, 17), for our times are linked inexorably to the fullness of God's Kingdom by the presence and power and wisdom of the kingdom's Lord and Messiah now.

If the Kingdom is present, i.e. if the destruction of the work of evil spirits has begun to be replaced by ever fuller life, we can find some resonance with this teaching in the two small parables Luke now introduces. If the kingdom is present, then we can understand more fully the parables of the mustard seed and yeast.

The Parables

A. *The mustard seed*

Jesus compares the kingdom of God with the growth of a mustard seed into such a large tree that the birds of heaven can come to nest in it. Looking at Luke alone, without reference to Mark (who earlier spoke of the smallest of seeds giving rise to the greatest of all shrubs or garden plants), the emphasis in the parable is clear: what begins as a seed becomes capable of hosting the birds of heaven in its branches. One must be prudent here, but it is true that in this picture there is no limiting of the birds: they are not described as 'some' or 'a few' or even 'a lot'; the number is not mentioned, which leaves the listener to imagine most any reasonable amount of birds he can — and perhaps more than he even imagines. What at first is one seed, the smallest seed, becomes the home of countless beings — and a welcome home at that.

B. *The yeast or leaven*

Luke begins this parable with the words, "And again he said". Certainly, 'again' reminds us of the act of speech, that Jesus speaks once more. But it also carries to the content of this parable, that what Jesus taught through the picture of the mustard seed in full bloom, he will now teach through the picture of flour affected by yeast. In this parable a woman 'hides' yeast, but works it in such wise that it, though hidden, makes three measures of flour rise. Remarkable! a tiny piece of yeast produces such a stunning result, and in secret! Notable in this parable is an aspect not visible in the parable of the mustard seed: the woman works the hidden yeast and flour till all the flour has risen. In this parable, we have a picture of something 'hidden' which, over time and with work, influences what, without yeast, would remain unleavened. Finally, we can note that the image of yeast leavening 'all three measures of wheat flour' suggests something small creating a large fullness. Put more dynamically, the one piece of yeast, though hidden, has the energy to bring all the flour to its absolute fullness — again, if someone will work it.

C. *The two parables teach*

Taken together, the parables underline how elements which are small, a seed and a bit of yeast, produce things over time that will, on the one hand, harbor many, many beings, and, on the other, reach its fullest and most complete growth, if only someone will work it.

Jesus has defined his public life's mission as 'announcing the Kingdom of God' (Luke 4, 43). With this central purpose of his life in mind, the parables of mustard seed and yeast are well understood to refer to the beginnings of the Kingdom of God which, over time and with the work of the proclaimer, will grow into the fullness of the Kingdom of God. In accord with the parables, the Kingdom will grow to embrace all peoples, and will have the energy to affect all peoples — if one will proclaim untiringly. Indeed, Luke wrote the Acts of the Apostles to detail how exactly the untiring work of Jesus' witnesses help create the Kingdom of God, create a tree to hold all peoples, to work a small message so that it influences the world.

Conclusion

We have noticed the likely connection Luke has drawn between the curing of a crippled woman and the dispute about it and the two parables of the mustard seed and yeast. When all this is seen together, one can understand how that cure/dispute story leads into the two parables, and how the two parables help make ever clearer the cure/dispute story. The cure of the woman indicates the beginning of the Kingdom, which, on the one hand, will grow to embrace many, many believers; the cure also will, through the indefatigable efforts of Jesus and others, bring to fullness, completeness what otherwise would be lifeless. But the Kingdom is not just begun, and developed over time, through healings. The Kingdom also is a kingdom where truth is clear. Thus, the words of Jesus, as they reveal the true mind of his Father (consider his correct understanding of God's will in the case of the Sabbath cure), are signs of the presence and influence of the Kingdom. Like the fruit of the mustard seed and the energized flour, the words of Jesus will reach many, many people and bring them to the fullness of their beings. Again, there is no question that the fullness of the Kingdom has not yet arrived, but there is also no doubt that Jesus thought he initiated that Kingdom, and that he, by deed and word, was bringing it ever closer to its perfection. His is a mission of joy, full of promise and full of hope. It also is as yet incomplete, for now God waits for people to accept His call to do the work involved in leavening the people of God's world and offering a home to all nations.

7. THE LOWEST PLACE (LUKE 14, 7-11)

Introduction

Luke presents Jesus at a Sabbath dinner offered by one of the leading Pharisees of an unnamed town, a town on his route to Jerusalem; Jesus, the Gospel reports, often eats with this type of guest, for especially do they like to have him present to test his wisdom about the Law. At this dinner Jesus noted at one point how some of the dinner guests immediately sought out the best or most honoured places at the dinner. Their taking the best places gives rise to a teaching of Jesus, a teaching in parabolic form that has as its subject "choosing places at table". What does he mean to say to these people?

What he says is clear enough, especially if one has gone through the humiliating experience of being forced out of a front row seat to a lesser, more distant seat, so that some one more 'honored or deserving' might have the better seat, suitable to his dignity and worth; measured by that person, you certainly do not merit being in that seat, but in a lesser one. You drop back humiliated.

Obviously, given this particular audience's perceived greatness of itself, such a fall from honor is indeed humiliating. We are asked to remember that honor or pride or dignity is a supreme value of the Mediterranean world of Jesus' time. Some societies are able to shrug off such a 'humiliation' — for them such a descent is not humbling at all. But in the world of Jesus, one's honor is one of the most important possessions of a human being; indeed, to appreciate the teaching here, a teaching which hinges on visible honors, one has to remember that often honor is for many the most prized possession, even more than money or beauty or talent.

The question is why did Jesus recite this parable? It was the audience who 'made him do it'. Consider the context. The dinner to which Jesus has come by invitation got off to a rather poor start. He cured a man with dropsy; more to the point, it was a cure of a man on a Sabbath (14, 1-6). Jesus' fellow guests, Pharisees and legal specialists, consider this cure as disobedience toward the Mosaic Law and its traditions. Curing was defined by the legal experts as 'work', and work was forbidden on the Sabbath. No pious person (and no one of Jesus' fellow guests) would attempt healing on this day.

Jesus' argument in favour of his 'work' is based on the fact that no one at the table would refuse to raise up a fallen ox of his on the Sabbath. Is not raising an ox, which has fallen into a well, a 'work'? Yet you allow such a work to be done on the Sabbath? Luke presents a challenge by Jesus to Pharisees and legal specialists: having cured a man on the Sabbath, Jesus asks about the legality of his healing, "Is it lawful to do good on the Sabbath rather than to do evil, to save life rather than to destroy it?" In other words, what does the Law of Moses say should be done on the Sabbath? (This story, in c. 14, is not a repetition of the cure of the bent-over woman of c. 13. In c. 14, the question centers on 'legality' of cure, whereas in c. 13 the question centers on the 'necessity' of curing a child of Abraham.) In our present story, the only outward answer to Jesus is silence. Inside, though, tempers rise. Once again, Jesus is challenging his guests, calling into question their claim to know the Law far better than he does. By out-arguing them he humiliates them. They have no choice but to concede his position — and such a concession is galling and a loss of face.

Note that it is not this humiliation which leads immediately and directly to the parable. What does lead directly to the parable is Jesus' observing, as Luke tells us, how the guests all sought out the highest, most honored places — whether they deserved them or not. By itself this homey parable seems to be simply a kind of social advice given to these social climbers. That Jesus spoke these words suggests, however, that he means us to find spiritual significance in them.

We know Jesus is not concerned with improving one's tactics at gambling for the right seat — a balancing between taking as high a place as one can get and running a risk of being taken out of it. Given what Jesus has just experienced, however, in his exchange with the specialists and Pharisees about Sabbath practice, the parable is very timely. Jesus' cure and argumentation lead to the subtle teaching, which our parable proposes very cleverly, that, though these guests, led by Pharisee and Scribe, might try to hold onto exalted positions in society, it is Jesus who has supplanted them, and they must yield with humility to him. In short, the teachers who had the best seats, those of teachers of the Law, now are the students in the lesser seats who must yield the best to the best teacher. To save themselves public humiliation, they should admit without struggle the superiority of Jesus' teaching and learn to abide by it. Eventually the Gospel makes clear that their refusal to accept the authority of Jesus' teachings goes beyond humiliation; his teachings are one of the root causes why they had Jesus killed.

A further teaching at this same banquet, and following the parable, again shows how differently Jesus and his fellow guests think. Jesus asks that, when you offer a Sabbath dinner like this one that he attends, out of respect for the meaning of the Sabbath, the dinner should be open to the poor, the lame, the blind and the crippled. Those four categories of Jews point up the universal love of God for all Israel when he saved Israel from Egypt. All Israelites should be able to celebrate together on the Sabbath, their common heritage as brothers; there should be no restriction according to such wrongful motivation, 'who will invite me in return', or 'who is of my station in life'. The unity of Israel is mirrored on the Sabbath Day: all Israel should in principle be together. Is this expression of unity such a heavy onus? It should not be. Indeed, if I ask about obligations (like Sabbath) owed to God, God has made it abundantly clear, both by His own actions and by His command to love one's neighbor, that the Pharisee and Scribe, indeed all Jews, should embrace one another and live in signs of this love. The Sabbath Day dinner is a particularly opportune time to show this universal love of neighbor.

The point, then, of the parable comes clear when we consider all that transpires at this one Sabbath dinner in the presence of Scribes and Pharisees. Humbling though it may be, to recognize one's place, whether vis-à-vis the wisdom of Jesus or the dignity of the poor, is to know one's proper place — and knowing one's proper place will cause no humiliation, but only glory to him who knows who he is and where he belongs.

Perhaps above all other parables, context seems to be the key to interpreting a parable of Jesus.

Conclusion

The brief parable, in which Jesus warns his fellow guests about the danger of taking a table place that is above their merit, seems solely humanly prudent in its advice: choose the lesser seat (or the right one), to save yourself possible public embarrassment. One looks for a spiritual meaning in this piece of advice. Certainly, the parable ends with an aphorism to be found elsewhere in the Gospels (cf. Luke 18, 14, and Matthew 23, 12), "Everyone who exalts himself will be humbled, and he who humbles himself will be exalted."

But in those places the contexts make clear the spiritual meaning. Luke 18, 14 sums up the fact that a sinner (a tax-collector), having confessed his unworthiness, is forgiven or raised up, whereas a Pharisee, with no admission of sin while contemning his brother, remains unforgiven or humbled and humiliated. Matthew 23, 12 speaks to the fact that a Pharisee and Scribe, who are hypocritical in presenting themselves as falsely charitable, will be humbled and the one who serves others in charity will be raised up or honored. But, in our parable, to what fact does this saying, exalting and humbling, refer?

Jesus gives the parable while watching people try for places at table which they do not merit. They will be humbled; whereas there is good chance that they may be raised up, if they are in a place lower than where they should be. The one to decide, however, if one has placed himself above or below his station is not the person himself, but God. All depends on His reading of my innermost soul.

While one might be satisfied with this analysis of the parable, I thought it would be better to give, as with Luke 18, 14 and Matthew 23, 12, a concrete example of pride, of coming to know one's proper place. In this vein I have appealed to the story immediately preceding our parable. It is, as explained, a story of both miracle-working and contestation (a mix of two different literary forms). A key idea is that the pious and generally acclaimed wise teachers of Israel cannot respond positively and humbly to Jesus' interpretation of the Sabbath; their silence can mean only that he is right and they are wrong. In the story they remain in seething silence. But it is clear, too, that apart from anger, they are humiliated and Jesus is exalted. It would be wiser for them to know themselves and their proper position vis-à-vis the correct understanding of the Law they purport to know. They were the teachers, the honored ones; with the presence of Jesus, they become, unwillingly, the students, the humbled ones. They should know their place, as Jesus does his. If anyone is glorified in this contestation, it is Jesus, who begins suspect, but finishes with a display of wisdom beyond that of the host and his other guests.

As mentioned earlier, at this dinner Luke has more lessons for the Pharisee and his guests than just this parable; Luke has a number of points to make here, and some of them are in another parable about a meal, that of the refusals of certain people to come to the Great Banquet (14, 15-24). Perhaps it is not by chance that these lessons, for the Pharisee and his like, occur midway through the Gospel; this placement might mean that Luke wants Jesus' conflict with religious authorities of his time to be a central and pivotal theme. Certainly, they are prominent in the material Luke has chosen to use in his presentation of Jesus' journey to Calvary and from there to the right hand of his Father. But these are just some of the lessons Jesus has to give to the religious leaders of his time; there will be others. Luke thinks it best to repeat these confrontations to Theophilus and his community. They certainly go ultimately to explain why Jesus was crucified, but they may also be lessons needed to be learned by the Christian community of Theophilus.

8. God's Invitation Scorned (Luke 14, 16-24 [15-24])

Context

Jesus is in the house of a leading Pharisee; it is a Sabbath, and after the Sabbath liturgy, a dinner is underway. In this meal situation, and before the parable, Jesus first cured a man suffering from dropsy. This cure, because worked on a Sabbath, called for justification, since curing on the Sabbath was forbidden — it was designated a 'work', and working on the Sabbath was sinful, against the Law.

Then Luke reports that Jesus, still at the dinner table, offers a wise bit of advice. Choosing the lower place offers the possibility of being honoured or glorified by being given a higher place — he implies that, should one not be offered a higher place, he does not lose face, but remains in a seating right for himself. On the other hand, choosing the higher place offers the possibility of being humiliated, for it may be made clear in public that one does not deserve the higher place, but only a lower place. If this advice is considered wise among men (and who at the table would think it not wise?), they should accustom themselves not to take stations in life they know they do not deserve — and who, before the all-knowing God, will take a place he does not deserve? Jesus' advice to his fellow guests is that they should take the lower places at the table, for, as often happens at dinners, and always happens before God, the humble (who admit their failures; cf. Luke 18, 13-14) will be exalted and the proud (those who exceed their true value before men and God) will be humbled.

At this time of a Sabbath meal, one is always reminded of one's neighbors; care of the poor — of all Israel — is a meaning of the Sabbath. On the Sabbath, one is expected to show honor and love toward all Israelites. Thus, Luke (with vv. 12-14) also notes Jesus' remarks to the host of the Sabbath dinner: one fulfils the Law of God, not simply by showing friendship to those who can be of reciprocal help (sinners do that), but to the poor, the crippled, the lame and the blind, who, by definition, can be of little or no reciprocal benefit to a benefactor. Jesus' fellow guests must learn to think beyond their own circles of friends, to care for every one of their neighbors as they want to be cared for. One does not ignore one's friends, but one does not ignore the less attractive and the needy, either, for God has enjoined this love of neighbor on us — especially on the Sabbath.

All of the above points are 'eye-openers'. They are revelations to guests, to these people who do not think as Jesus thinks. Indeed, they do not think as their ancestors did. Though there are examples enough in the Jewish Tradition which support Jesus' teachings here, his fellow-guests do not live in this way. From another point of view we can say that in accord with his calling people to repentance, Jesus is here giving beneficial, concrete teachings about just what the repentant person will think and do.

Introduction to the parable

At a certain moment in this dinner situation, one of the guests makes the comment, "Blessed is the person who eats dinner in the Kingdom of God"; probably what made the guest at this moment think of this blessedness is the preceding reference to the equivalent of the Kingdom of God: "the resurrection of the just". One has the suspicion that this guest might think of himself as one of those 'just'; is he? This pious remark leads now to the fourth and final lesson to come from this dining occasion. There is no doubt that the words of the guest are true: blessed be the person who eats in the Kingdom of God. What the man means, of course, is that one is blessed who gets to enter the Kingdom; eating there is just one of the signs of having passed the crucial Final Judgment — but who will that be?

As often happens, Jesus builds on someone's observation as a spur to give more of his teaching. In this case, Jesus offers a lengthy parable, aimed particularly at the kind of audience with whom Jesus has associated himself (Pharisee and friends); a group which needs this particular parable. It is a group which does not understand the relative value of Sabbath observance in relation to love of neighbor, which seeks honours even beyond what is just and which has little concern to love, to associate with the poor, the lame, the crippled and the blind. After the parable, will the man who talked about blessedness understand better what is needed to enter into the Kingdom and attend its banquet? Will he understand what it takes to merit being called 'blessed' in the Kingdom?

How to understand this parable?

This parable is deceptive. That is, it is not easy to know when to apply the elements of the parable to real life, and when to leave elements of the parable in the fictitious world of the parable. Of course, when one has read the parable, one can say with confidence that Jesus is speaking about refusal of God's invitation, an invitation through Jesus, which refusal results in not eating of the Lord's banquet. Indeed, as elsewhere in Luke's work, the last line here — I tell you that none of those invited will taste my dinner — offers the teaching of the parable. In other words, accept My invitation, or come not into My kingdom. (It is worth noting now, and later, that the Gospel tradition looked forward to a heavenly banquet called at times God's banquet and at other times the Messiah's banquet.)

But granted the simplicity of the parable's message, there are a number of moments when one is tempted to see in fictitious details of the parable references to real life — and thereby understanding Jesus' view of life. But do all the details of the parable mean to be interpreted as referring to one's life with God? Upon reflection, we find it is difficult to move as freely as we might want from fiction to reality. Let us consider these problem elements. It is often said that Jesus did not allegorize; it was later generations and centuries that allegorized. Yet, this parable is from the start pushing the reader beyond the normal circumstances of a human (albeit fictitious) situation to see, from the beginning, the world of God and of rejection of His call to prepare for Judgment.

Circumstances involved in Jesus' parable

A. *The invitation to the dinner*

We have to think that the three guests of the parable have already, before the parable begins, been invited to the banquet; otherwise, the announcement that "things are ready" seems, at least in the human situation, very foolish. No, the guests have already learned of and been invited to a banquet; they just do not know the day and hour of the banquet. The parable begins at a second moment, the moment when a notice of the readiness of the banquet is now sent to the already-invited guests. Probably, at the first invitation the host did not say when the second notice would be sent; he expected these guests to hold themselves in readiness. In this case, the invited guests should be ready at any time to receive notice that 'everything is ready: come!'.

Perhaps one feels that the host is expecting too much of his guests, "to be ready whenever I call". But this parable, as so often with Jesus' teaching in general, is aimed at teaching readiness for God's call to Final Judgment. What might prove unrealistic in our social world is not so in God's world. There one does know that he is invited to the heavenly banquet, but does not know the precise date of that banquet, and so should hold himself ready for the call at any moment. Jesus has elsewhere taught that we should be ready at any and every hour.

In the world of God, think of the insult given to Him if an invited guest, knowing that he should come to the Final Judgment sometime, so involves himself with other things that he cannot be ready for it; clearly 'other things' are of more importance than the banquet. One will hear shortly the tragic words of Jesus, "Just as it was in the days of Noah, so too it will be in the days of the Son of Man. They were eating and drinking, and marrying and being given in marriage, until the day Noah entered the ark, and the flood came and destroyed all of them. It will be the same as it was in Lot's day: people were eating and drinking, buying and selling, planting and building, on the day when Lot left Sodom, fire and brimstone rained from the sky to destroy them all" (17, 26-29). One should know, Jesus contends over and over, that there is a Judgment to pass in order to enter into the

Kingdom and share in the heavenly banquet — and he teaches so also here. The cavalier attitude of the three invitees suggests a situation similar to Noah's time: they had 'other things' on their minds, and were in no way ready for salvation. The ancient situation and the present one are situations that arouse God's anger.

Thus, the parable calls for readiness to come to the dinner, even if, contrary to what happens on the human level of the fictitious parable, one does not know the time of the final invitation; in God's world, the real world, one knows he will be called and that he cannot ignore the call. Another tension in comparing the parable to real life is the fact that in Jesus' teaching there are two calls one must heed. The latter, the one to face Final Judgement, is what we have talked about so far. The earlier call is that of Jesus to repent; repentance is now, in preparation for the Final Judgement. Both these calls can be part of the parable: the parable prepares for the final calling, but also supports Jesus' present call to repent. But then, the depressing frivolity and negativity of this rejection scene corresponds to the negativity which defines the parable: no one of those invited will eat My dinner!

B. *A wedding banquet*

We cannot identify with certitude the kind of 'great dinner' talked about here; yes, many would suggest a wedding banquet, but that is only a guess. But why this guess? Because the banquet of the Kingdom of Heaven is often described as a Wedding Banquet, and since Jesus apparently means that his audience interpret this imaginary banquet as the Heavenly Banquet (My dinner), some scholars feel justified in calling this dinner a wedding event — the type of the glorious Banquet to which we all are called for eternal life. Put another way, if the banquet be the Wedding Banquet of the Jewish Scriptures, this detail suggests that Jesus means to call upon those feelings which have spurred every Jew over centuries, focused on participation in this wonderful banquet; the Book of Revelations (the Apocalypse) takes this wedding banquet theme as a major image in its teaching. Indeed, Jesus likens himself to the bridegroom: "Jesus answered them, 'Can you make the wedding guests fast while the bridegroom is with them?

But the days will come, and when the bridegroom is taken away from them, then they will fast in those days'" (Lk 5, 34-35). (In Jesus' applying to himself the title of 'bridegroom', one senses a mystery: in Jewish writings only God had been identified as the 'Bridegroom' of Israel.)

On the human level, the intensity of the host's anger is better understood; from his point of view, these invitees are refusing to attend what is to him a very important event; he thinks they should have kept themselves ready. His prospective guests had been asked and have shown themselves uncaring and preferring other things, indeed disparaging the kind and lofty invitation. The intensity of God's anger is even more understandable, for this is the eternal Banquet about which Jesus speaks, the only and ultimate Banquet of eternal happiness. What is more important than it? With due distinctions, then, the concept of Banquet is an element which one can transfer from the fictitious world to the real world.

There is a certain strain on credibility in the story, for it is not altogether clear why, if the invitations had gone out according to custom, the recipients would not have been ready to receive them. The suggestion has been made that the invitees mean to insult their host, precisely by attending to matters of lesser value than his banquet, when they indeed were, or should have made themselves free to attend. The suggestion has merit, but the text of the parable does not adequately support it.

C. *The excuses*

We are to understand that the first two excuses are rather weak, not at all justifying the great snub the invitees offered to their prospective host. Why weak? Their tasks — visiting one's newly acquired field or oxen (both already acquired) — hardly need to be done only on the day of the banquet and on no other day. And while being newly married has its own obligations, it is difficult to understand why these obligations prohibit attendance at a banquet which had already been agreed to by one knowing his wedding date, or at least promising to hold himself in readiness for the call to the banquet. And even though one recognizes that the human banquet (a wedding banquet) in Palestine of this day lasted some days, this excuse is really flimsy; these excuses explain the sense of anger on the part of the host — can any of these activities be of more worth than participating at My banquet?

Other parts of Luke's Gospel, as well as teachings from the Jewish Tradition, focus on the absurdity that human beings ignore the call of God, or have become too crass to hear it, because they are absorbed in the things of this human world They are concerned about such human activities as farming and buying new properties and marriage — they do not want to disturb this human rhythm with thoughts about readiness for the Final Judgment. It is worth repeating the quotation given above; though said on another occasion and in different circumstances, these words of Jesus fit well here: "…in the days of Noah, they ate and drank, they took husbands and wives, right up to the day Noah entered the ark — and when the flood came, it destroyed them all…in the days of Lot, they ate and drank, bought and sold, they built and planted, but on the day Lot left Sodom, fire and brimstone rained down from heaven and destroyed them all" (17, 26-29). "Be ready" is an essential plea of Jesus. Once again, in considering the three excuses Jesus cites in this parable, one already feels drawn to the real world where human beings ignore the call to that repentance which leads through the Final Judgment to the Heavenly Banquet, and prefer to concentrate on other things.

D. *The one servant*

Throughout the entire parable there is only one servant used by the host to bring his words to designated invitees; this servant may be the one always charged with the office of 'convoking'. Yet it seems strange that there is only one servant involved. Perhaps the 'great dinner' is not so great after all? But a glance at Matthew's version of this parable will find that many servants are involved, not just one. Indeed, it is extraordinary that only the one servant cover all points mentioned: the broad streets and narrow alleys, the by-ways and hedge rows outside the city walls, to 'bring in' more new guests to the banquet. One cannot help but think that Jesus is here allegorizing: 'his servant' is Jesus. As the imaginary host is a figure for God, so the imaginary single servant who carries out the will of God is Jesus. This 'divine' meaning of the parable explains what is very unlikely on the human level. (Matthew's version of the parable was noted just a moment ago; there, we find reference to 'many servants'. Since their services are in the past tense, it is clear that these servants are the Old Testament prophets, who culminate in Jesus.)

E. *"Go to the broad streets.....Make them come in."*

When one reads such a biblical phrase as 'to broad streets and narrow, to the poor, the crippled, the blind and the lame, to by-ways and hedge rows outside the city walls', one has met up with the biblical style in which the idea of 'everywhere' is spelled out in many concrete instances of place and people. Thus, 'Go anywhere and everywhere, and to all kinds of people' and bring them in. The banquet will be enjoyed by all. Again, we have an allegorization built into the parable. The action of the fictitious host may seem odd to Jesus' listeners: why would the refusal of the invitees warrant the participation of people not at first allowed (and never, in the parable, invited) and of the lowest classes?

Given the unexpectedness of the fictitious host's orders, one suspects, and rightly, that Jesus' audience is here, as elsewhere expected to move immediately from the imaginary to the real world. In the real world of Luke, one looks back over the past fifty years or so that have passed between Jesus' time and Luke's time. In that look, one sees three facts: 1) Jesus (according to Luke's Gospel) preached only and on principle to the Jews, not to the Gentiles; 2) while a good number of Jews believed in Jesus, and particularly right after Pentecost, a very significant number did not; these refused the invitation to be ready to enter the Kingdom of God; 3) however one explains it, the invitation to the Gentiles to come to the banquet was issued after the life of Jesus, after the refusal of his own generation. Only in the Acts of the Apostles, and not at the beginning of it either, do we find a wholesale effort to include Gentiles in the Wedding Banquet.

These three historical points sound very much like, and correspond to two major points in the fictitious story: 1) an invitation to one group, and 2) an invitation to others only after the refusal by the first group. Thus, we have a first account of an invitation to a particular group which means to focus our attention on Jesus' call to repentance among his own people, and we have a second account of an invitation to others, apparently people who became Christians in the decades after the public life of Jesus was over. What Jesus expects, then, from those who hear his parable is an understanding that, 'should you refuse Me, I will invite others, and you will be left out'. Here we have another case of the fiction pointing to a reality.

Notice that it cannot be by chance that the very same groups are mentioned in this parable as were recently mentioned in the verses prior to the parable: the poor, the crippled, the blind, and the lame. While they fit well as fictitious characters in the parable, they also reflect realities of Jesus' time, of every time. Clear attention to them can only reinforce the conviction that Luke wants to underline, here and in so many other Gospel moments, the importance of these people in God's eyes — they too will be brought, however one explains the timing of their call, to the Banquet.

F. *Two problems*

First

The parable so posits the invitations to the first group that one can conclude that if this group had accepted their invitations, no invitation would have been extended to anyone else. If we transferred this thought from fiction to reality, it would mean that if the Jews of Jesus' time would have believed in him, no preaching would have been done to others (Gentiles). Granted the logic internal to the parable: acceptance of one invitation would eliminate any further invitation. Certainly this seems a right interpretation of the fictitious situation presented in the parable. But, if we move to the real world, is Jesus saying through the parable that God has worked, or would work, in this way? If the Jews had accepted Jesus, God would not then have preached to the Gentiles?

Such a conclusion in the real world contradicts the entire Lucan story, and indeed a major portion of Jewish teaching, and so cannot be retained.

An answer is that this suggestion, that invitation goes to the Gentiles only if Israel refuses Jesus, cannot be sustained by history. What history has shown is that the invitation did go first to the Jews and then to the Gentiles, but it does not show that the invitation to the Gentiles completely depended on the rejection by Israel. Let us look at Paul's thought, for Luke valued it and Paul's theology was already known broadly in the Mediterranean at least 20 years before Luke wrote. Paul had often said, "To the Jew first, then to the Gentile", but he did not mean by this "To the Jew, and then by default to the Gentile". It is true that a hallmark of St. Paul's understanding of God's will was that he should go always to Jews first, and only then to Gentiles. And the Acts of the Apostles consistently indicates that Paul's going to the Gentiles occurred because of a first refusal by Jews. And Paul himself, in Romans 11, 17-25, describes the removal of those branches from the olive tree root, which makes room for the insertion of wild, unnatural (non-Jewish) branches. Particularly, Paul's word reminds us very much of the teaching of the parable that "my house must be filled": "blindness has come upon part of Israel until the full number of Gentiles enter in" (v. 25). But, to repeat, neither Paul nor Acts argues that the Gentiles were to come to the Heavenly Banquet only because certain parts of Israel had refused God's invitation; such a thought never enters into the New Testament. It was always God's will to incorporate the Gentiles into this Banquet, but the incorporation was to follow the sequence, first to the Jews, then to the Gentiles.

Neither did Jesus indicate this kind of 'by default' thinking in his life; he certainly went to the Jews first, but never denied that God always wanted salvation for the Gentiles, too. We must note, too, that Isaiah had long before Jesus said that the Gentiles would come to worship God together with Israel; but he did not say that the Gentiles would come only if the Jews rejected God. Thus, there have already been indications in Scriptural teaching that resonate with the teaching of our parable: it will be a banquet of many kinds of invited people; the invitation will go to Jews first. But Scripture does not agree with the parable's suggestion that 'others' will come only on condition that the first invitees refuse to come.

We conclude then that the thinking of the parable's host, that some will be called only after others have refused, is not to be transferred to real life. Yes, the calling of one group precedes the calling of another group, but the second calling does not depend on the refusal of the first — in real life. One recognizes once again the allegorization built into the telling of the parable.

Second

"My house must be full". This is given in the parable as one, if not the motive for further gatherings of people after the first were rejected. Does it reflect only the mind of the fictitious host or are we to learn from this that God's motive in calling people to His dinner is simply that "My house must be full"? Now it is true that at certain points in the Old Testament we do find God acting for Himself. At Psalm 106, 8 the Psalmist says that "He saved them (rebellious Israel) for his own sake, to make known his power". But the overwhelming evidence, both of the New and Old Testaments, is that God calls to His dinner because He loves those whom He has called. Thus, it seems best to say that the motivation that moved the host to invite the second and third groups ('to fill my house') is not to be understood as that which moves God to call all people to the Wedding Banquet; with the parable we are already in the mode of allegorizing.

G. *Anger at rejection*

Perhaps it is good to address here the image of the host as angry. Is the host's 'anger' a description of God? Is the anger of the host meant to be not simply fictitious in a parable, but real in real life? There is a long history of the attitudes and temperaments God has revealed about Himself. The Old Testament shows God to be not only kind and merciful, but also angry — particularly with anyone who does not adore Him alone; God is jealous, and anger follows closely upon jealousy. Well over 40 times in the New Testament is God described as angry. St. Paul will say, in the first chapters of the Letter to the Romans, that what characterized God's feeling toward the world before Jesus was anger; this anger changed only with the death and resurrection of Jesus. In short, it is easy to see in the picture of the fictitious angry host a description of the real God. Jesus himself does not shy away from describing God as very capable of anger. Of course, it is another matter, a matter for theological reflection, whether God is ontologically a Person of emotions, but Scripture presents Him that way.

H. *Emphasis of the parable (v. 24)*

The second and third callings (vv. 21-23) are not detailed at all as is the first (vv. 18-19) — particularly there is no account of acceptance or rejection by these groups, or even of invitation. This argues that they are not really a main concern of the parable. Within the logic of the parable, only the first invitation is the invitation that matters. One can see this from Jesus' final words. He speaks, not of those who were brought 'to the Banquet', but of those who refused to come. The parable is not about the successful acceptance of the invitation, but about failure thereof. It is this message that Jesus wishes to convey to his fellow guests around him. Blessed indeed is the man who eats in the Kingdom of God, but woe to him who does not accept the invitation to this dinner! Thus, the parable is a 'threat-parable', and its chief tool is not what later groups did, but what the first group will suffer for refusing the call to the Wedding Banquet.

Indeed, we never want to lose sight of the fact that the parable is told to a specific group (who, among other faults, ignore the poor, the crippled, the blind and the lame), that the world is viewed from the point of view of their future judgment; the parable is capable of application to others, but this parable in organized really only for a specific kind of person. With this in mind, we consider the mention of a second and third group of invitees to be secondary; as noted, they are not handled in the parable with the attention given to the first group, and it is worth noting again that Jesus' ultimate words concern only those not allowed to taste his dinner. This factor makes it difficult to identify and/or separate the second and third groups — are they sinners? are they gentiles already converted to Judaism? are they pagans? If one compares Luke's parable with the same in Matthew, we see a difference: the third group is unique to Luke's parable. This third group is considered by many an addition by Luke, meant to bring the call to the Banquet beyond Israel and its outcasts to the Gentile world. This may be true and, if so, valuable for understanding the parable. But the concern is not with them, but with the first group; it is this group that is the focus of Jesus' parable.

I. *Notable parallels*

One of the ways to decide what in the parable is to be transferred to real life is to see if the teachings of the parable correspond to other teachings Jesus offers elsewhere. We have seen examples of this principle already: God's anger is taught outside the parable, as is the singular role played by the one servant; too, there is ample evidence that Jesus' fellow dinner guests, like all Jews, know of the Banquet of God — this banquet is not simply fictitious, proposed for the purposes of an imaginary story.

There is a particular example from Jesus' preaching that helps interpret the view Jesus expresses in our parable. We recall its salient points.

Luke gives the question asked of Jesus, "Lord, will many be saved?" (13, 23) In answer, Jesus brings up the image of a householder who at a certain point shuts his door and thereby leaves out 'those who can truly say that "we were with you and you taught in our streets"' (v. 26). Upon closing the door on his acquaintances, Jesus employs another and religiously traditional image, that of Abraham, Isaac, Jacob and the prophets of Israel. They will be in the Kingdom of God, but "you, who have heard and seen and touched me, will be left outside" (v. 28). Finally Jesus moves from the children of Israel to those who "will come from the east and the west and from the north and the south and will recline at table in the kingdom of God" (v. 29). With these verses already in the reader's mind, we find the direction of the parable clear, namely, that those who refuse him will not be present at his dinner — ironically, others who are not from Israel, and from elsewhere, will be.

The parable of Chapter 14 clearly reflects an earlier teaching (Chapter 13) of Jesus; this earlier teaching helps us understand the thought embedded in the parable of Chapter 14.

J. *The call — in the story and in real life*

Luke introduced our parable with the words of one of Jesus' fellow guests, probably one who thinks himself to be worthy of a blessing: "Blessed is he who dines at the banquet of Heaven". The parable of Jesus identifies who will not eat at this banquet. It will be those who refuse the invitation of the one Messenger or Servant. Jesus means to say that to enter the Kingdom and participate in its Banquet, a person must accept the present call of Jesus to a repentance which will allow one to be ready for the final call to enter into the full Kingdom. As he will say later, 'Now that I am here, everyone is mightily urged to enter the Kingdom of God' (16, 16).

We noted earlier that the parable seems to assume that a first invitation has already been issued to the prospective guests; they are already invited. In real life, the audience of Jesus — particularly these fellow dinner guests — knows of the heavenly Banquet. A person does not know when the Wedding Banquet of Heaven will take place, but a person knows, first, that it will come, and second, that he must hold himself ready for its coming, that he must pass the Final Judgment. One knows that nothing will be more important than that moment when one receives the final call. One cannot prefer other things to this Banquet, and one cannot fail to prepare oneself for the Banquet.

But to consider Jesus as the servant of the parable means that we emphasize the call to repentance, that is the trademark of Jesus' purpose in life. But as Luke has presented Jesus, this call is a consequence of his greater mission, to announce the Kingdom of God. Thus, Jesus' call to repentance is a call to come to the Banquet. In realizing this, we realize again that, while the call of the Servant Jesus occurs now, the moment of Judgment will occur later, perhaps much later — certainly not, as the story presents the matter, within a few hours of the call. Too, the Final Judgment occurs once and so all attend together, but the length of time for repentance can occur at different times, not at all at the same time for everyone. We can say that it is with a clear eye on the future that one repents, and the sooner, the better. Indeed, the Christian feels the tension between 'now' and 'then', as he waits for many years for the happy conclusion to his life of repentance, which is more according to real life than the attention only to the future call to Judgment which is suggested to us by the parable. A concrete awareness of this relationship between the call of Jesus and the final call to Judgment is an essential element of Peter's hallmark discourse at Pentecost. He notes that 'anyone who calls upon the name of the Lord will be saved' (Acts 2, 21), (a favourite saying in the decades after Jesus' life). He means that one calls NOW, one calls on the name of Jesus NOW, in order to be saved in the FUTURE, at the future judgment. As a result of our considerations throughout this discussion, are we far off if, in the light of the entire Gospel and Acts, we recall that there are really three calls in the real world of God: the call to the Kingdom at the beginning of life, the call to repentance in mid-life and the call to come now to the Banquet.

We are saying, then, that the call of the parable, so immediately preceding the celebration of the Banquet, must be nuanced so that one understands that Jesus, Servant, calls now for that change of life which will lead to passing the Judgment and entering into the Banquet.

Zachary, the father of John the Baptist, offers a clearer description of what will happen at the coming of Jesus, the divine Power of Salvation: "he will save us from our enemies so that we may NOW worship God in holiness and justice all our days" (Luke 1, 69. 74-75). Zachary makes clear that salvation leads to a holy life NOW, and that one is not saved only after one passes the Final Judgment — all the more an indication from Luke that, while the Servant Jesus is understood to call us to the Judgment, he is the Servant in real life who calls us to a human life of repentant living till we are face-to-face with the Final Judgment and, then, enter into the Wedding Banquet.

And when Jesus calls to repentance, he is thinking particularly of his most recent words to this audience at table with him: he asked that host and fellow guests attend lovingly to 'the poor, the crippled, the lame and the blind'. Jesus agrees wholeheartedly that "to love God with one's whole heart and mind and strength and to love one's neighbor as oneself" is the principle which guides all moral actions; this principle, clearly enunciated in the Old Testament, is the backbone of Jesus' moral teaching and of his own choices. We need not run through the many teachings of Jesus in this regard in Luke's Gospel, for it is clear, even in a quick reading, what he thinks is the essential principle of human action. Love of neighbor is the expression of repentance and the way eventually to pass the Final Judgment.

Conclusion

It has taken us awhile to draw out a complete meaning from Jesus' parable about God's invitation scorned, but we can very briefly say that, granted the internal logic of the fantasy story, the reality the story means to describe is the rejection by God of those fellow guests of Jesus who have refused His invitation, an invitation delivered by Jesus, to enter the heavenly Wedding Banquet. That others will be at that Banquet who were not among the first invited — that is true, and Christian history is witness to that fact. (The call to 'others' is not dependent on the refusal of the first; that is an element of the parable which is not meant to describe God's actual plan of salvation.) But the story begins with Jesus' fellow guests and is aimed solely at them. It is from their perspective that Jesus speaks about 'others' participating in the Banquet of Heaven while his fellow guests do not. God will be angry at these people around Jesus who refuse his call to be blessed in the Kingdom by repentance now. They should not be surprised, and their own Scriptures give witness to this, that others will be at that Banquet and they will not. Luke, even while anxious to assure Gentile Christians of their entry into the Heavenly Banquet Hall, respects Jesus' concentration on his own fellow guests and the tailoring of the parable just for them. As it was Luke's task for his own time, it is now the preacher's task to move from this concrete answer to a particularized Jewish audience to an audience which is centuries away and in so many other ways different from the original audience of this parable.

9. LOST SHEEP, LOST COIN (LUKE 15, 3-10)

Introduction

A. *Hearers of the parable*

As Luke's Chapter 15 gets underway, we meet three 'personages': 1) tax-collectors (always considered thieves) and sinners, 2) Pharisees and Scribes (specialists in the Mosaic Law and its traditions), and 3) Jesus. The first group 'listens to' Jesus; in Lucan language that means they are listening favourably to his words, and suggests perhaps an inclination to change their lives. The second group grumbles; their complaints center on the fact that Jesus receives sinners and eats with them. No doubt they are thinking that Jesus is breaking the Mosaic tradition which forbids close contact with sinners, a contact such as eating with them and receiving them (as though into one's home). These two activities, eating with them and receiving them, are points of contestation on a number of occasions in the New Testament, especially as, later, Jewish Christians begin to win over Gentiles to faith in Jesus.

To 'them' Jesus offers a parable. The 'them' refers to some people indicated in the first two verses; most likely, the word refers to the Pharisees and Scribes who find fault with Jesus, but a case can be made that the word includes both sinners and Pharisees and Scribes. Both can profit from the parable of Jesus.

Jesus tells 'a parable'. What we read is two parables, one having to do with a lost sheep and the other having to do with a lost coin. Evidently, it is the close likeness (even in wording) of each parable to the other that allows Luke to describe them in the singular: a parable. (On the other hand, Matthew knows only one parable, that of the lost sheep.) Actually, Luke will add a third parable of Jesus with v. 11: it is the parable of the Lost Son. Because we treat that parable in a section of its own, we pay no attention to it here, but, if one reads that section, he will see that we felt we had to include a treatment of the parables of lost coin and lost sheep when speaking of the lost son.

B. *Notable elements of the parables*

a. Neither parable is concerned about how a sheep or a coin came to be lost; the point of each parable is not in that. The point is simply that they are indeed lost. This is quite unlike the parable of the lost son, which for a number of verses depicts the young man as very much in the throes of sin. One can see why this third parable, having to do with the Prodigal Son, is quite distinct from the first two parables having to do with a sheep and a coin. The third parable is seen to appeal directly to the sinners to whom Jesus is in part directing these three parables.

b. That a shepherd leaves his ninety-nine sheep and goes after one is not to be misunderstood; we are not to think that by going off to search after the lost sheep, he endangers the ninety-nine. There would be no point to his concern for one which would lead him to be unconcerned about the many and so eventually bring him to search, not just for one, but now for ninety-nine! The audience of Jesus, so attached to the Land as they were, would understand, without further word, that the shepherd would leave his ninety-nine only if they were safe.

c. The emphasis meant in the question, "Who would not leave…?", means to underline the fact that certainly a shepherd would leave the ninety-nine — which is another way of indicating the worth of even one sheep. Jesus does not mean to imply that the one sheep is worth more than the ninety-nine, but that even one is worth all the effort of searching and searching and searching until it is found.

d. The problem with the parable (and it is the same problem with the parable of the lost coin) is identifying the teaching(s) of the parable. There is the theory that a parable should have only one point to make, and so we should look for one point in Jesus' parables; if there is more than one point found in the parable, it surely is inserted by another person than Jesus. But it is such a theory that makes interpretation of this parable (and that of the lost coin) difficult. Is there only one point to these two parables? We will propose two, while at the same time asking how these parables might challenge both sinners and the pious teachers.

Two emphases of the parables

As mentioned, 'lost' is only a circumstance of the story; it gives rise to the two results that the parables highlight.

A. *The one who searches*

First, there is the picture of the one 'who searches and finds'. In each case, the searcher/finder works hard to recoup something of value. It is the value of what was lost that causes this hard work. A sheep is worth a great deal, obviously, and the coin lost is, in Jesus' world, equal to at least one day's wages, and particularly valuable since the woman possesses only ten such coins. In both stories, the finder is such that he or she will not stop searching till what is lost is found. As the parables implicitly ask, "Who would not keep searching till what was lost is found?" Both shepherd and woman work ceaselessly; moreover, the shepherd, once he finds his sheep, carries the lost sheep on his shoulders — a sign which signals the tenderness of the shepherd for his sheep, which, again, is thus revealed as more valuable to him than just money. Finally, we note that the searches described, one in the desert and another in a house, take the searchers to 'anywhere the sheep or coin might be found'.

What can we learn from these parables so far? Most clear is the evident, ceaseless efforts of the shepherd and the woman. They are to be esteemed, for the audience is asked to identify positively with them: "Which of you would not do what they do?" Moreover, in regard to the animate sheep, the tenderness the shepherd shows his inner feelings which help motivate his continual search. Finally, the two, shepherd and woman, will go anywhere to find what they value. This certainly is one of the meanings of the parables when placed within the purview of the two classes of people which are introductory to them.

Lesson for tax-collectors and sinners

How will the sinners who hear these parables react? Will they understand better that Jesus is unremitting in searching for them, untiring because he has tenderness toward them, goes anywhere if that will help find them? Are not the parables signs to the sinners to look carefully at who encourages their repentance, signs that should help allay the fears, including fear of an unloving God, that accompany the first tentative movements towards moral change? Will one not find courage when it is such a caring person who wants only to find what he and she esteems so highly? Will one not put one's trust in such a person? (Because of the particular attractiveness of the shepherd-sheep parable, it can be called the more important parable, to which the story of the woman-coin is added for emphasis; this subordination may justify the use of the singular, 'parable'.)

Lesson for Pharisees and Scribes

And the Pharisees and specialists in the Law? Should they not be able to see that the efforts of Jesus, which take him to anywhere he can profitably encounter sinners — that these efforts constant and untiring, and are motivated by the esteem, and love, he has for these sinners? Can they argue with his intentions to bring people to convert, no matter what it takes from him? The Pharisees and Scribes complain because they only see the most visible: Jesus eats with sinners and receives them. But if these social moments result in repentance for sins, how can they continue to fight Jesus — after all, the repentance of sinners certainly proves the legitimacy and value of Jesus' kind of searching; as Jesus noted earlier, "Wisdom will be proven right by her children"; the results will justify the means (7, 35). There is always the question of the possibility of breaking the Law of Moses and its traditions; but Jesus understands that the Law is subordinate to his mission, that the

Law of God is meant only to help, not hinder the return of His children to God. In subordinating the Law and its traditions to his mission (i.e. the traditions as interpreted and taught by Pharisees and Scribes), Jesus, if he continues to live this way, will die for his belief. Will the parables make any clearer both the reason why Jesus associates with sinners and why his association with them is in accord with, and not against, the will of God?

B. *The joy at conversion*

A second emphasis of the parable: in each story a good amount of time is spent describing the joy at finding what was lost. In fact, so much of each story depicts the joy and almost excessive celebrations that follow upon the findings that one is tempted to see here the point of each parable: not so much of concern here for the effort spent in searching, but of the rejoicing that follows upon finding. Again, one must concede to the stories that what their central characters, shepherd and woman, seek is something of very great value to them. This value not only explains their unceasing efforts, but justifies the extreme joy each experiences at his and her success.

Lesson for sinners and tax collectors

And what will be the effect on sinners who hear of such joy over the finding of what is thought to be so valuable? What does this say to them about their own worth? Joy characterizes heaven itself when one repents; the state of repentance must be, then, a joyful state and not what many sinners fear as an unhappy existence. This joy, on earth and in heaven, is the signal as well that one has avoided the punishments due to sin. The sinner is subtly reminded of these punishments when heaven is said to know only joy at the sinner's repentance. Strictly speaking the stories of shepherd and woman need not have continued after notice is given that they found what they had lost. But the stories do continue, and that makes us think that, as far as the sinner is concerned, he should know both the untiring love of the searcher and how much the searcher values what was lost, and the eagerness to rejoice that follows upon the findings. Both the figure of the searcher and the joy of what is now found — both of these elements are enticements to the sinner to repent.

Lesson for Pharisees and Scribes

The Pharisees and Scribes, too, must understand not only the eagerness of God and of Jesus to search whenever and wherever to find what they think worth every effort, but the immense joy experienced on earth and in heaven at the finding of the sinner. Never lose sight of the goal, suggests Jesus; repentance is met with joy and the Pharisees and Scribes know this well. Let them keep this in mind lest they focus only on the infringement of laws and not on the supreme importance of the search for sinners — which after all is a concrete expression of the Law everyone agrees to: "You shall love your neighbor as yourself". These people must learn to love even sinners, and not despise them.

Conclusion

The parables of lost sheep and lost coin can, and should, appeal to both groups listening to Jesus. The parables have messages for both groups. Ultimately, the goal is repentance in regard to the sinner and cessation of animosity towards Jesus in the conduct of the Pharisee and Scribe. In regard to the latter, there must be a better understanding of the Law or mind of God; so often the difference of opinion about the centrality of certain laws, e.g. of Sabbath observance, is at issue in Jesus' public life, as is respect even for the sinner. Sadly, the full Gospel shows that Jesus' view of the Law of Moses was never accepted, nor was his authority to interpret it. It is a very telling part of the third parable, that of the lost son, that this parable has no actual ending: what did the elder son do, after hearing his father's explanation for his actions? Will the elder son see things the way his father does? This is an ending, too, for the first two parables: will certain Pharisees and Scribes see things the way Jesus sees them? Clearly, sadly not. But the sinner should take heart in the picture of the efforts Jesus expends to find them and the joy

Heaven shows at their finding. In their finding lies the joy of the Gospel.

A footnote

In the first parable it is said that "there will be more joy in heaven over one sinner who repents than over ninety-nine righteous people who have no need of repentance" (v.7) . To some, this seems to be an unfair evaluation. Is it? First of all and at least as a start of an answer, it is clear that the entire New Testament and the Jewish Scriptures know only of a great joy in heaven over all the righteous people, the saints. Second, given the extreme likeness between the parable of the sheep and the parable of the coin, it is notable that in the second parable there is no repetition of the statement as we find it in the first parable. There certainly is emphasis on the great joy in Heaven at the finding, but no comparison made. This suggests that the formulation in the first parable is not essential at all to the teaching of the story; in the light of the second parable, it seems sufficient to underline simply the great joy of Heaven at the finding of what was lost. Jesus has no particular use now for the comparison he used in the first story. (From a synoptic criticism view, one might say that while the shepherd parable inherited by both Matthew and Luke has one formulation about joy in heaven, Luke changes that formulation when he is freer to report the story of the woman and the coin.) Third, in virtue of our second point, one realizes that Jesus' phrasing having to do with 'more joy' has more of a function of emphasis upon the full joy of Heaven at the repentance of the sinner, and so understands it as an example of a manner of Jesus' speech which is visible elsewhere in his teaching: it can be called 'exaggeration', i.e. exaggeration to make a point; Luke would have understood the parable as containing this exaggeration. Fourth, as the circumstance suggests, the 'greater joy' is momentary, lasting as long as the gathering of friends lasts; as such it suggests no unending time like eternity.

In short, in regard to the phrase 'more joy', we interpret the first parable by the second, and we give priority of meaning to the second over the first. It is hard to deny that Luke does too, for he has put the two together of his own accord and called the two one parable. He is not unaware of what he is reporting, or intending a wrong sense as its understanding. If he is comfortable with his presentation, we can be too.

10. PARABLE OF THE PRODIGAL SON (LUKE 15, 11-32)

Caution

As introduction to the Prodigal Son parable, we recall that, on the one hand, Jesus is being listened to favourably by sinners and tax-collectors (thieves) and, on the other hand, is being criticized intensely by Pharisees and Scribes because "This one receives sinners and eats with them" (Luke 15, 1-2). These contrasting reactions to Jesus are what move Jesus to give his three parables about 'lost and found'), the third of which (after sheep and coin) is the famous parable of the Prodigal Son. Eventually, we will have to look at the parable from the perspective of these two introductory verses; they will help us interpret the parable as Luke wants it interpreted. (We will consider the parables of the Lost Sheep and the Lost Coin at another time.)

Some clarifications

A. *Between father and younger son*

Jesus spends time describing the wasted life of the younger son. The audience cannot but recognize this life to be a tragedy — all the more so because he had the wherewithal to have an enjoyable life. The most evident degradation is summed up in his willingness to eat the carob pods which usually were feed for pigs.

Unlike the shepherd and woman of the previous two parables, this parable does not depict the father as going in search of his lost son. On the other hand, we cannot ignore the fact that the father has been looking out for his return: "While the son was still far away, the father spied him"; moreover, the father ran to meet his young son, embraced him and kissed him (Luke 15, 20).

Jesus' brief, poignant descriptions mean to strongly contrast two figures: one, who wastes money he has not earned, makes terrible, degrading mistakes and nearly destroys himself, and the other, who ever watches for his son' return, and, upon seeing him coming home, knows only to be compassionate, to run and embrace and kiss him. How much more contradictory can two people be?

The young son deserves little credit for coming home. His reasoning clearly shows his self-interest, the same self-interest that has guided his life all along. There is no desire to see his father, but only to eat better than what he is eating now.

There were generally two kinds of servant in this world of Jesus. One lived in a village and came to and from work every day and night; the other lived in the house of the master. It is the former kind of servant that the son asks to be; he realizes he has no call on living in his father's house again. Let him live from a salary, and not enjoy the benefits of the old home.

The speech the son prepares expresses an awareness of sin; perhaps we are to understand that he is implicitly asking for forgiveness. What he explicitly asks for is servanthood.

It is no surprise that the father does not let this son finish his prepared speech; the father has only one reaction to his son, and it is not to consider him a sinner. How does he think of him? As one who was dead and lost, and now alive and found.

Jesus focuses attention on the father now. The father follows up on his emotional welcome with four gifts. He gives his newly found son the best garment available, a ring and shoes. In a household all of these things indicate the wearer to be a member of the family, indeed, a son and not a servant. Finally, he orders a banquet to be celebrated and the highlight will be to eat of a calf which has been nurtured for an eventual great feast.

At this point, the audience, both audiences, should understand the reactions of the father; do they approve of it? The father defends himself from any implicit criticism: He who was dead is alive; he who was lost is found. Jesus' audience, any audience must evaluate the father's actions, especially against his stated reasons for those actions: dead now alive, lost now found. The father has no intention of punishing his son who has, granted, a minimal change of heart; elsewhere and in other contexts, Jesus will definitely speak of final punishment for sins. At this moment, in this parable, Jesus has made clear that the son was terribly wrong, a sinner; he makes equally clear by omission that punishment is not on the mind of the father, but only joy at the son's change of heart and return. Will the sinners in Jesus' audience understand that they are dead, but have the possibility to be alive? Will the Pharisees and Scribes think the father foolish in his apparent gushing over his disreputable son? Will they begin to think about sinners as does the father?

B. *Between father and elder son*

Jesus now turns his attention to the elder son, indicated in the first verse of the parable: "A certain man had two sons". Notice how the relationship reported now is solely between father and elder son; certainly, the younger son stands behind the discussion of father and son, but Jesus concentrates directly only on the latter two.

The circumstance which occasions the discussion between father and elder son is that with which the story of the father and the younger son ended: the banquet of joy over the son returned. In a sense this banquet and the associated gifts, which express the will and intention of the father, are the literary lynch-pin of the lengthy parable. Joy which ends the story of one person begins the story of a second person.

Once the elder son has understood the meaning of the sounds of joy and celebration, the scene is set: your brother has come, your father has killed the fatted calf (a sign of an extraordinary banquet) because he received his son in good health.

Are not Jesus' hearers expected to rejoice with the father? Such is not the reaction of the elder son; he is angry and refuses to participate in the banquet. Once again, the father moves, not this time to receive a returning son, but this time to plead with his elder son. It is the father who extends himself, to each son in his own way, trying to help each see the situation as he does and accept that.

The elder son now explains the somber position he has taken. For me who has always been faithful and obedient — there has never been a banquet like this, and for this person (called 'your son', not 'my brother') who has wasted all your money, for example on prostitutes — to him you give a wonderful celebratory banquet. What is the justice when the obedient has no reward and the disobedient enjoys the father's best things?

The father's answer, with which the story closes, is twofold. First, the elder son must not forget, in his thinking about this momentary banquet, that "You have been with me always, and all I have is yours". How the audience evaluates this argument is important: what is the value of fidelity and life with the father? And what is the value of a dinner, however wonderful, that is ephemeral? Does one not realize how far more valuable is the meaning of "all I have is yours" than a dinner? Indeed, the argument is immeasurably bolstered because precisely what the elder son has enjoyed 'always', the younger son, in his wasted life, never has enjoyed, and never will; nothing can make up for a life lost in evil, lost because 'he, unlike you, has not been with me always'.

Second, the father, so much better than the elder son, realizes what the return of the lost son means. What was dead is alive, what was lost is found. Does the elder son realize to any degree what the father realizes to the fullest degree? Who sees the reality better: father or son?

The reader's past education in literary expression might suggest that death-life be in the place of emphasis, i.e. the last place in the sentence; death-life should follow lost-found, for there is nothing more drastic than the chasm between life and death. But because this parable has been joined with the previous two, in which there is no return from death to life, but only finding what was lost, this third parable is adjusted to end with the now threefold message: what was lost is found. Undoubtedly, however, the definitiveness of death and the total return to the greatest gift God can give, life — this is the most precious meaning of a person returned from sin.

What did the elder son do? Jesus does not say; he is content to finish with the saying, "What was dead is alive, what was lost is found". Apparently, Jesus left the remainder of the story to the judgement of his audience, the sinners and the religious authorities. For Jesus, it is most important to understand the father, to underline the reasonableness of his actions, to perceive things as he does. Neither son realizes what Jesus' audience is asked to realize — therein lies the lesson of the parable.

Sinners and Pharisees hear this parable

As mentioned earlier, we must return to the first two verses of Chapter 15 to grasp fully how Luke interprets this parable. These two verses indicate that the explicit audience of Jesus is sinners and tax-collectors, on the one hand, and Pharisees and Scribes, on the other. What should be the effect of the parable of the Prodigal Son on these two groups?

Such an introduction as Luke has used to introduce our parable suggests that the parable is meant to show how Jesus appealed to the sinners, on the one hand, and to the religious leaders, on the other. We know, from the Gospel, that Jesus "came to call sinners to repentance"; further, we read how many stories Luke retained for his Gospel that had to do with correction of Pharisees. Into this life-long struggle of Jesus, to call and to correct, we find explanation of the Prodigal Son parable.

The picture of the prodigal son, the full picture, is meant ultimately to be an attraction to repentance or conversion. Sinners can identify with the young son, and admit what many of them in a number of secret moments know: they have wasted their lives and turned their backs on their Father. Sin brings one to eat like the pigs. Repentance brings one sonship, undeserved and unmerited, but sonship, and deserves to be marked by a wonderful celebration. Indeed, the Father has forgotten about failure, he only knows and cares that what was lost has been found, what was dead is now alive. It is not by chance that the Greek word which describes the sinners as "listening" to Jesus really means, whenever Luke uses it, "listening favourably". The sinners are not sceptical of Jesus; they know deep down that what he says is true. The offer of a life of full joy (which is what the sinner is after anyway) is a powerful attraction drawn from the experience of the Prodigal Son. Finally, sinners will admit that, once they have found true life, they will forever regret not enjoying it always.

The Pharisees and the interpreters of the Law of Moses approach Jesus from a mix of feelings. On the one hand, they are described in the Gospel as jealous of Jesus. But, on the other hand, and more importantly in relation to the parable, is their conviction that Jesus is entirely wrong in his approach to sinners, and indeed by it flaunts the teaching of the traditions of Israel that say: 1. to associate with sinners is to open oneself to becoming one of them ("one bad apple...") and 2. to associate with sinners is to blur their own awareness of the horror of their sins; indeed, stay away from sinners, so that they learn from a frigid society the severe error of their despicable ways. We should assume that Pharisees and Scribes, at least in theory, are not against conversion of any sinner to a life of true obedience to the Law of God. But these religious leaders will tell us that their experience of sinners makes association with them dangerous to society and insensitive to their own sins. They clash with Jesus in this matter. What is at stake in Jesus' treatment of sinners is the long-standing tradition, based on experience, which we have outlined.

With the parable Jesus means to justify his actions by virtue of the well-known principle that the end justifies the means. He should be judged, he thinks, not by the tradition or experience of others, but by the result his association with sinners produces and by his own perpetual sinlessness. It is for these opponents to show that Jesus has committed wrong with his approach to sinners, while at the same time realizing what the results of repentance and forgiveness, as he preaches it, will be. That is, it is difficult to quarrel with the father and side with the elder son when one comes to the end of this parable; the fact is that the lost son is home. One can only say to Jesus: good luck, bring them home in whatever way you think you can.

A final note in regard to what the father says to his elder son — and by extension to sinners and pious alike — is important. To be with the Father is to have everything the Father has; to be with the Father who has everything is to have everything. Poor sinner who, for whatever amount of time, is not with the father and therefore cannot ever be said to share in all that the father has.

The proper title of the parable

We all know this parable to be the 'Parable of the Prodigal Son'; some people prefer 'sinful' to 'prodigal' because not everyone today has 'prodigal' as part of his working vocabulary. This classic title suggests one of two things: either 'prodigal son' is only a way of introducing the parable, since it is the prodigal's story that does start off the parable, or 'prodigal son' is the parable's character that the listeners should give most attention to. Certainly, over the years the sad state of the prodigal, and then his repentance, has occupied many a lesson and homily aimed at having the sinner turn from sin, repent.

Though there has always been a strong, vibrant current in Christianity which underlines the mercy of God and God's joy at a sinner's repentance, more so in the last couple of generations has this current been emphasized. In line with this conscious emphasis, attention has turned to the actions and attitude of the father and results in the question "Is it not true that the merciful father is the major character of the story?" Indeed, from a literary point of view, the father seems to be the one who links together the other two characters of the story and holds everything together. Without the father, there is no forgiveness or banquet or joy. And, without the premise of the father's expression of joy over his returned son, there would be no explanation for the reactions of the elder son and the sublime answers to him. Indeed, one could argue that the prodigal son only serves to show the depravity of sin and leads to the joy over repentance, and that the elder son is only used to show the ignorance of a person who does not appreciate a life spent 'with the father', does not realize that with repentance what was dead is alive and misunderstands Jesus. From all that we realize is said through the father, we could entitle this story the parable of the Joyous and Merciful Father.

Yet, the third character might deserve to figure in the title of the parable; the Elder Son has a truly significant role to play. True, it is his opposition to the father that helps make clear what is the reality perceived only by the father, that a human being had been lost and is now found, has been dead and now lives. But the Elder Son is more than simply a literary foil for the father. His angry question goes beyond the parable and is heard over and over again through the centuries after Jesus, "What about me, who have served you faithfully and not sinned; what value is that?" — or, again, "How can he, that sinner who wasted everything on prostitutes, be rewarded better than I?" If the thinking behind those questions is important, then so is the figure of the Elder Son. Should one read the parable with the realization that everything is leading up to the confrontation between father and elder son, and to an answer to the perennial questions: Why should I obey? Why should the sinner be rewarded more than I?

Also, it is true that, whereas the story of the prodigal son has its (joyful) ending, that of the elder son does not. We wait for this son's decision. Which in turn means that we wait for the Pharisees and Sadducees to make their decision about Jesus. Will these religious leaders, in light of his successes, agree to Jesus' approach to sinners, will they stop their murmuring against him? Will they even admit that Jesus does reveal how God thinks about sinners and about the just? The entire Gospel will give an answer to these questions, and not the parable. Indeed, the reader must give an answer as well.

It probably is enough that the traditional title of the parable remains as is: the Parable of the Prodigal Son. But it is clear that the title cannot hide the variety of teachings in this one story or even anticipate them all. All the values of the parable should be esteemed and preserved.

Conclusion

Whatever might be an appropriate title for the parable, the parable is meant to speak to those represented by the two other Gospel 'characters', the sinners on the one hand, and the pious on the other. From this point of view, one sees that it is Jesus' intention to speak both to the ugliness of sin and to the spite of those who want to stop his ways of calling sinners to repentance. To them both, each in his own way, he says: do you realize what it means to be lost and then found, to be dead and then alive? This question is at the heart of the parable and utmost in the mind of Jesus. From this it seems to follow that the central character of the story is the father, since it is only he who conveys to the listeners the reason why Jesus assiduously searches after lost souls and the reason for the immense joy upon one's conversion - indeed, a matter of life and death, from death to life. The hearer of the parable might agree with the prodigal son, "I am not worthy to be called your son", and can understand the view of the elder son, "I have always done what you wanted, but you give me nothing equal to what you give the sinner", but these thoughts give way to the profound understanding of the father; he is the only one who understands and defines reality, tells it "like it is": sin is a matter of death, repentance is a matter of life, and blessed is he who brings the sinner to life.

11. THE PRUDENT MANAGER (LUKE 16, 1-8 [1-13])

Introduction

It is no surprise to anyone that an estate owner, be he in the first- or twenty-first century, would periodically ask for an accounting concerning the financial well-being of the estate entrusted to the manager he has hired. It is the moment after the owner has asked for this accounting that is the concern of our parable. We will hear from the master of the estate in vv. 1-2 and v. 8; the desperate thinking and clever actions of the manager, which form the basis for a judgment, make up vv. 3-7.

A. *The beginning of the parable — the master*

It has come to the hearing of a rich master that his manager has misused (technically 'scattered', then 'wasted' or 'squandered') the master's possessions. It is not stated precisely what the manager did wrong, only that he did do wrong in the matter of his master's possessions. Later, in v. 8, the owner confirms this wrong when he calls the manager (literally) 'a manager of injustice', i.e. an unjust manager. There is no quarrelling with the fact: the manager has done evil. The owner asks for an accounting: if it turns out badly, as the rumor had it, the manager will be fired.

B. *The center of the parable — the manager*

The focus of the story moves now from the master to the manager; there is no pretence that the manager will be able 'to balance the books'; implicitly, he is admitting his failure to manage properly. We are now at the heart of the parable: the manager must think how he can come out of this problem safely; he surely will be let go, according to the direct words of his master — and then what will he do?

Here we have the famous line, "To dig I am not able, to beg I am ashamed" (v. 3). So we listen to hear what the unjust manager will do about his future, the right decision. It is here, in this steward's moment of enlightenment, that we find the center of the parable. The manager's solution is to reduce debts owed to his master. To one who owes 'a hundred measures (eight hundred gallons) of oil', the manager says, "Take your bill, and sit down quickly and write fifty". To another who owes 'one hundred kors (a thousand bushels) of wheat', the manager says "Rewrite the promissory note so that it says eighty". With this report, the manager ceases to be at the front of the stage; he yields that dramatic and literary place to the owner from whom we now hear. Before thinking about the owner's words, however, let us consider two ways in which we might understand the maneuver of the manager.

The purpose of the manager's reducing debts is to find places (and people) who, out of gratitude for his actions, will take care of his future. What precisely has the manager done when he reduces these debts? For many scholars, his actions are cavalier and wrong; he is again misusing his master's goods, indeed clearly stealing from him ("Don't worry, just pay for 400 gallons of oil; don't worry, just pay for 500 bushels of wheat"). His illegal and immoral acts here suggest what explain why he is being let go by his master (v. 2): he scattered (to others) what the owner possessed. Thus, the manager thoroughly merits the title of 'unjust', the title about to be given him by his master (v. 8). Indeed, that the manager is called 'unjust' immediately after his desperate decisions suggests to many that it is particularly these present decisions, on top of the earlier squandering of the owner's goods, which merit him that description and thus show these particular acts to be cheating.

Some scholars will suggest another way of looking at the matter. For them, one is first to consider that the manager, in Jesus' time, knew that part of his income from his master will be from the debts people paid to the master. Thus, the manager knew that some of the value from a debt of eight hundred gallons of oil will be given to him, and some of the worth of a thousand bushels of wheat will be his. With this in mind, could we not say, the argument goes, that all the manager is doing is yielding to these debtors his own income, that he is not, in the long run, cheating his master? Whatever one's choice in the matter (the majority opinion or the minority opinion), it is clear that the description of the manager central to the parable is that he is unjust; if he is not unjust from his immediate transactions, he was unjust in squandering his master's possessions. It is this description with which we must work in the parable.

C. *The conclusion of the parable*

Now it is time for the owner to react to his manager's activity. Notice that we never hear what actually transpired from the actions of the manager; did he find a safe haven in his future? What is crucial here is the observation of the owner, called here 'the lord' of the estate (some scholars understand that 'the lord' is Jesus): how clever is my manager!

We can only insist on attending solely to the cleverness of the steward, and on nothing else that might describe or concern him; we can only agree with the master that the manager, unjust as he certainly is, has acted cleverly in his own regard. Many who read this parable understand the master to be praising the manager without due regard for the evil the man has done: for them there is the problem, "How can the owner praise an unjust servant?" But to ask that question shows that the questioner has not grasped the precise (and only) point of the parable: the cleverness of a person in regard to his future, or, if we may put the matter in a more religious vocabulary, prudent choices in regard to his salvation.

The End of the Parable

Verse 8 has been a problem for interpreters. Only a few scholars say that the parable ends with the end of v. 7 — which means that, for them, the 'master' who, in v. 8, brings out the lesson from the manager's actions is not the fictitious master or lord of the parable, but Jesus himself, the Master, the Lord. This reading does not mean to change the correct understanding of what Jesus wanted us to learn from the actions of the manager, namely prudence in making choices for salvation. It only raises the secondary question, did Jesus continue the parable through at least v. 8a, so that the master or lord of v. 8a is still the fictitious person of the parable, or is Luke reporting from outside the parable that Jesus the Lord (v. 8) is drawing the proper conclusion from the parable (ending with v. 7)? There is no universal agreement among scholars about the identity of the 'lord' of v. 8a, but the large majority of scholars hold that the parable ends with v. 8a.

But the effort to put an ending to the parable has led to the suggestion of some scholars that the parable ends only with v. 8b included, that the fictitious master explains, indeed, that the children of this age are shrewder, more astute in dealing with their own generation than are the children of light (in dealing with religious matters). This, too, is a possible part of the parable, though it seems to add an awkward length to v. 8a. Again, other scholars will give this explanation to Jesus speaking outside the parable; in this interpretation Jesus himself (not the master) would be explaining the previous words of praise for the manager's prudence. Again, it is still a disputed point among scholars with the majority favoring the ending of the parable with v. 8a.

Verses 9-13

For the moment, let us follow the theory that we finish the original words of Jesus with v. 8a, that the rest of v. 8 is spoken, not by the fictitious owner, but by Jesus himself, for in referring to 'the children of this age' and to 'the children of light', Jesus has shifted from the economic language of the parable to terminology most at home in Jewish religion. (Recall that to be 'in the light' was a very old, long-time description of Israel, who had the presence and the mind of the one true God, and the pagans, who, without the true God, knew only darkness.) Thus, the lesson of the parable is the demonstration of cleverness in securing one's future, a cleverness that the disciples (to whom the parable is told) should exercise even more, since their future to secure is their salvation. A first observation about vv. 9-13 is in order. We are not saying that they were not spoken by Jesus; rather we are saying that they were not part of his original teaching on the occasion of his giving this parable. Then, too, vv. 9-13 entertain the thought that some of these verses may not be not words of Jesus, but interpretations of his parable by later preachers, interpretations which Luke, under the inspiration of the Holy Spirit, knew to reflect the mind of Jesus and a true meaning of the parable. Finally, vv. 9-13 can be understood to represent verses said separately and at different moments and later gathered into a type of catalogue that makes them appear to be said all at the same time, as we have here.

Verse 9 is a conclusion drawn from both the parable and from v. 8. The wily manager can be said to have made friends through his reductions of debts. He has shown them how beneficial he can be to the debtors; surely the debtors owe him something now. This 'new friendship' is an example that "You, too, make sure that when you die, you have 'made the friends you need' (=obeyed God) to have eternal life".

Verse 10 is a proverb-type saying; as such it can serve in a variety of situations. Here in Luke's Gospel it is meant to underline the logicality and inevitability that go with being faithful in little things — certainly such a person can be trusted with greater things. Not so the evil person! The sinful, evil manager is a good example of one who by being unfaithful in little things, has proved that he will cheat in greater things. Certainly, one can understand this proverb in a restricted sense: a person who is unfaithful in a smaller church position will prove untrustworthy in a situation of greater responsibility. Such a lesson fits well with the developing need for leaders in the Christian communities existing throughout the Mediterranean Basin. Too, the parable makes one recall the truth within the Scriptures that grace from God will be all the more if one proves him worthy of this "more" ('to him who has, still more will be given' Lk, 8, 18). Perhaps, though, we are ultimately (though imperfectly) talking in spiritual terms: fidelity to God in this life will move God to give me the greatest of gifts, eternal life with Him, a gift which is wholly incommensurate with my obedience on earth. In this last suggestion is missing what is in the proverb: if one is faithful in little things and so gains Heaven, he cannot be said to "be faithful in heavenly things".

Verse 11 means to be a conclusion from the general statement of v. 10 which distinguishes between 'those faithful in little things' and 'those unfaithful in little things'. The 'things' now are limited to one type of 'thing', namely the use of what is dubbed 'wicked mammon'. Mammon was the name of an evil idol of the pagan world, thus an insulting alternative to the true God. In v. 11, as generally at Jesus' time, by the iniquitous mammon is meant money, worshipped as god and used evilly. In Jesus' teaching, money is in itself good. But he calls it evil because in his experience it is so very often used in an evil way. For him, what guides the use of money is the principle from which should be derived every human moral act: 'love of God and love of neighbor'. Often he found that money took on the aspect of god, for in so many cases it is money which is adored, and in money one thinks to find his salvation. If one cannot be trusted to use money well, why should he be thought to use well the things of 'eternal and divine value'? Why think that people who use money badly will use things of true value well?

Verse 12 concludes a reflection on the trustworthy, on those to whom one cannot entrust things (ever present in the background is the experience of the master and his evil, untrustworthy manager.) Here, too, we have a particular conclusion from the general sense of 'things' that we saw in v. 10. 'Things' had been reduced earlier to 'money'; now 'things' is reduced to 'another's things'. Here we have a direct address to the audience, 'Would you entrust your things to a person who cannot handle morally the things of another person?' Perhaps the thinking behind this question is again the moment for choosing responsible leaders in later Christian communities.

In these three verses, 10-12, the conclusion to the parable focuses on 'the one who is trustworthy, untrustworthy', in accord with the primary defect of the iniquitous manager. Certainly, one can see the connection of these verses with what went before: they are reminders both of the 'children of this world' and 'the children of the light', as well as of the unfaithful, untrustworthy manager and his angry master.

Verse 13 is a continuation of the reflection begun in v. 12, about the place of God and money in a person's life. It points up the impossibility of adoring both God and money. If one gives the qualities of God to money, what use will he have for God? Conversely, if he gives the qualities of god to God, he will keep himself faithful to God and consider money as a means to reach God. It is impossible to obey both God and money, in the sense that only one of them can be God who commands obedience. Evidently, people have tried to worship God and money, and have tried to obey money at the expense of God and His Law. Is Luke' audience reflected in these verses?

Are we still in the realm of the parable? Has the wicked manager tried to adore both God and money? He certainly has, contrary to the will of God, put his trust in money for his future. To that degree he can qualify as a person about whom v. 13 speaks. Certainly, outside the fictitious world of the parable and in the real world of God, one can serve only God or money. It is Jesus' wisdom that says one cannot serve both — either we inevitably end up worshipping money or God; we can't do otherwise.

12. The Rich Man and Lazarus (Luke 16, 19-31)

The context

In the preceding five verses (16, 14-18), Luke has described the Pharisees as 'money-loving'. This description is meant to be harsh, intentionally so, for it is unusual, indeed not said of these people anywhere else in the Gospels or Acts of the Apostles. The heart of Jesus' complaint is that the great commandment, love your neighbor as yourself, is sacrificed to keeping one's wealth, and love of self, at the cost to one's neighbor, is preferred — and this is done by the pious Pharisees! Note how these verses, beginning with the topic of 'money-loving', flow easily, logically from the preceding parable based on the misuse of money (16, 1-8), and from lessons to be learned about abuse of money (16, 9-13). What we have here with our parable, then, is the continuation of a long consideration by Luke about the misuse of wealth (which, we might note, began with the Prodigal Son). Our parable will help clarify this situation. The Pharisees complain about Jesus' parable concerning money; Jesus now, in clear and strong language, argues his point (in favour of the proper use of money) against their anger with him.

The words of Jesus (16, 15-18) following this Lucan presentation of the Pharisees in v. 14 concentrate on what Jesus shares in common with his audience: great respect for the teachings of the Old Testament. There is only one way to enter the Kingdom of God(16, 16), and that is by obedience to the teachings of God, in this case about the right use of money (which, as used by the Pharisees, Jesus says, is hateful to God, for they have made it sacrilegious). The Law, which speaks about the right use of money, will never pass away; it is always, in all matters, to be the guide to human choices (16, 17). The only thing

Jesus adds to these venerable teachings of God is his own clarification about specific Jewish understandings of the Law of Moses (verse 18 is an example of this kind of clarification). The Christian is the one who, while recognizing the value of the Old Testament Law, lives that will of God according to Jesus' understanding of it. Indeed, the Christian responds to Jesus' moral teaching precisely because he is the teacher of it; it is on his word that our hopes are founded, not on those of Moses. Indeed he is not only our saviour, but also our guide and our enlightenment to lead us, through the best of moral action, into the Kingdom of God.

Given this lengthy five-verse preparation (which itself is a commentary on the 13 verses preceding them), we turn to our parable. Indeed, there is no word or phrase to connect it to the verses which precede it; one simply moves from vv. 14-18 without further addition by Luke — a sign in itself that the parable belongs very much with the verses that precede it.

Elements of the parable

A. *The rich man*

The rich man has no name; in Latin, the word 'rich' is dives, and so it happened that over the years the rich man was called Dives. Other suggested names derive from post-biblical copyists' and scribes' imaginations. This rich man is enormously rich. It is as though the parable's first line, which describes this man, runs too fast; we must slow down to appreciate the wealth of this man, and his consequent way of life, in order to understand the immense (even exaggerated?) contrast Jesus establishes between the rich man and Lazarus.

We adhere as closely as possible to the Greek text so as to appreciate what Jesus is describing. This man habitually wore purple and fine linen, celebrating every day splendidly. 'Habitually', and therefore not just on 'Sunday' or some other special day; he was habitually dressed in purple and fine linen. 'Purple' means a clothing, dyed at least in part in purple dye, for which one paid very handsomely;

the trade in purple dyes from such areas as modern Turkey was very profitable, so much so that only royalty or those of the highest class could afford to wear purple — and this man wore it daily! Similarly, we are speaking here not just of linen, but of fine linen, a rare item among the population even of Rome, and certainly not something most people would wear (or could afford to wear) even occasionally, not to mention every day. It was customary that a household have one main meal a day; in the house of this rich man, that meal was a celebration, a feast — every day. And it was a splendid feast, apparently one that could be recalled for its superior foods and drinks, its service and presentation. It is important to realize fully that such a celebration involved guests; the rich man did not dress as he did and present food as he did, just for himself.

We are given only one line and less than ten words that describe this rich man, but Jesus has painted an initial picture that would stick in the imaginations of his audience (and probably raise some jealousy and anger in some of his listeners). One might accuse Jesus of detailing a picture that is almost a caricature of real life. Even if this be so, his point will turn on what to do with an abundance of wealth and how such abundance cannot save, but serves to destroy its owner. It is the severity of the lesson that justifies the presentation of this fictitious rich man, to some degree present in everyone, whether in fact or in desire.

B. *Lazarus*

The opposite figure, to contrast as starkly as possible with the rich man, is a blind man. He does have a name and it is Lazarus, which means "God-helps" — a name which is significant for 'the blind and lame and crippled and poor' (cf. 14, 13 and 21). Of course, the question is: will the rich man offer Lazarus any help? The physical condition of Lazarus more accurately has two descriptions: he is blind and he is covered with sores. Lazarus needs friends to help him find food. They leave him at the entrance-way to the rich man's house, just about as close to the rich man as a poor, blind and uninvited person can get. And he is there every day. He could not be or remain unknown, whether to master or to guests, and indeed the fact that the rich man shortly calls the poor man in Abraham's bosom 'Lazarus' shows that the two are known to each other.

If there is any doubt as to the inner thoughts of Lazarus, Jesus eliminates it: Lazarus longed for even what might fall from the table of the rich man and his guests. In adding this point, Jesus is depicting for his audience a scene which usually consisted of the table participants who would wipe their fingers with wads of bread, then throw the wads on the floor, and little dogs that would eat the scraps that fell from the celebratory table. One imagines then that Lazarus seeks not to be among the guests, but among the dogs, so that he might have some food. Indeed, Jesus' picture includes the unwelcome image of dogs licking the wounds that inevitably plagued the blind man. Some commentators understand this licking as a way of dogs caring for the poor man; the rich man would do less for Lazarus than would the dogs. Equally, the licking by the dogs is often understood as no help, but a kind of animal attack on the helpless Lazarus.

Jesus' description of the rich man and of Lazarus ends here; i.e. the end is 'open-ended'. The contrast — even better, the contradiction - is clear. What will be the outcome? The lack of further description means that nothing changed all their lives long; each man continued, unchanged, to his death. What will be the lesson Jesus will draw from his stark, perhaps even exaggerated description of these two men?

C. *Hades, Abraham*

Jesus further draws another picture, this one of Hades. The scene includes a dialogue between the rich man and Abraham. The picture Jesus draws is noteworthy not only for the tragic aspect of a certain kind of existence of anyone in Hades, but also for the fact that nowhere else, whether in the teaching of Jesus or of the rest of the New Testament (or Old Testament), is there any indication that such a place exists as Jesus describes it in this parable. Many scholars conclude that the mixed picture Jesus offers, of suffering and consolation, is his one-time use of descriptions of tragic afterlife drawn from other Mediterranean regions (perhaps Egypt), but known to his audience. If Jesus chooses to talk about pain for sinners in the afterlife, he usually draws upon the experience of a city's inhabitants through the image of an everlasting fire on the city's garbage dump, perpetually lit to burn the city's refuse night and day, "'where their worm doesn't die, and the fire is not quenched" (Mark 9, 48; citation drawn from Isaiah 66, 24). Indeed, some scholars have over the years thought that the description of Hades in this parable is a description of a state which anticipates the final, eternal state of all; an argument in favour of this view is the non-presence of the Judge — all Abraham does is offer consolation and explanation.

We should note the characteristics of this Hades that Jesus has given us. First, the word Hades is drawn from the Greek world and its attempts to describe the afterlife of those who have died. For Greeks who thought there would be no resurrection from the dead yet immortality, the souls of the dead were described as roaming a sunless land, in a form which represented not their full and happy selves, but only an unhappy, forlorn 'shadow' of themselves; we take from this the term 'shadows or shades of the dead'. Even when resurrection from the dead began to be asserted in the centuries before Christ, life in the underworld of those awaiting resurrection was, even if without pain, bittersweet at best. In this picture Jesus gives, we find a person who is not just sad, but suffering, which is a bit of a stretch of the age-old image, (but not an unexpected one, given that some of these awaiting resurrection will be punished for their sins).

The rich man makes clear reference to his suffering in fire; particularly, it is his thirst which now is uppermost in his mind. He would be satisfied with just a drop of water — a stark contrast to the riches he had in life on earth. He looks up, for he is below — a symbol of his grief and humiliation, and a symbol of a neediness he cannot end by himself — a stark contrast to Lazarus, who wanted only scraps of food which he could not provide for himself, but is now exalted and in the bosom of Abraham, a place of loving contentment. A place of fiery thirst, of eye-contact, a great chasm that separates the consoled from the suffering — all of this is rather foreign to the Jewish images of the afterlife.

The appeal of the rich man is to Abraham, not to Lazarus. Other descriptions of Hades in ancient literature do not contain the figure

'Abraham, the Father of the Nations', the font of the children of Israel. His presence allows for a painfully sad language: the one calling for help is '(my) Father'; the one refused help is '(my) Child'. Even this cherished relationship cannot stop the fires and thirst of Hades.

Hades allows a suffering person to see another who is in joy. Lazarus had already been described in a way that reminds one of God's, of Jesus' unremitting concern for the poor and blind: at his death Lazarus was taken up by angels. Now he rests in the most intimate of places, in the bosom of his Father Abraham, which is a symbol in Jewish thought for the most intimate and desired place of union of two people: it is akin to 'heart to heart'.

The premise of the rich man's call to his Father underlines the essential unity that existed between the rich man and Lazarus; despite the immense differences Jesus has painted, Jesus makes clear that they are brothers, a relationship in ancient Israel which is difficult to describe for the implied closeness and love that exist (ideally) between the brothers.

Finally, Hades, we learn, has a chasm that cannot be bridged; certainly, not even Abraham can cross it. This is a symbol of the impossibility of change of reward and punishment, once this life on earth is over. This unchangeableness is one of the underpinnings in the almost desperate attempts of Jesus to have people 'change now'; we never receive any indication from the New Testament that the opportunity to repent will be given once one passes death. In fact, the rich man's concern to tell his brothers now about Hades suggests that after death there is no possibility for change.

The dialogue

The dialogue occupies most of the parable: it is a dialogue between the rich man, who begins it, and Abraham, who finishes it. Note that Lazarus has no active role in these moments of exchange; in fact he is a passive element throughout the story, and is no longer even mentioned, after verse 25, after which we still have six crucial verses to go! Could one do without the dialogue? That is, could one draw the right lesson(s) from just the stark contrast Jesus draws in his first four verses? No, and the main reasons are two: a) the impossibility of Lazarus coming to help the rich man is satisfactorily explained only here, and b) only in the dialogue does one have an understanding of why the rich man is in Hades.

The first four verses describe the ways of life and the deaths of the parable's two main characters. These verses set the scene, verses which call for interpretation. We are now to picture the rich man and Lazarus in their respective dwellings in the afterlife — one in Hades, one in the bosom of Abraham. What is not explained as yet in the parable is why the rich man suffers and why Lazarus is free of suffering. Their conditions in the afterlife are simply assumed in the parable as deserved. Abraham does not say that because the rich man had his goods on earth, he should suffer now; he only means to affirm the fact that he had them on earth, implying that beneficence does not follow him to Hades. It will become clearer, as one reads the rest of the Gospel, that both the rich man and Lazarus had to be able to pass the Final Judgment in order to achieve eternal happiness. Their previous, earthly lives are responsible for and are the causes of their conditions in the afterlife; for now, we assume that the rich man is suffering in accord with the divine will, and that means punishment for some serious reason. What is clear now is that whatever good things he might expect ever to have, he has had them on earth; after death expectations do not count any more, but good now follows only on certain evaluations of his earthly life.

The opening of the dialogue Jesus gives us is a plea for a mere drop of water. We have already noted the poignancy in this plea of a child to his Father.

A. *The first half of the dialogue (vv. 23-26)*

What occupies the bulk of the first half of the dialogue is the reasoning of Abraham as to why Lazarus will not help the rich man. Note, it is not Lazarus who offers the reasoning; it is the Font of Jewish religion, Abraham, from whom comes this teaching. It is fitting that the father of all of Israel explains why Lazarus can be of no help now to the rich man. All the children of Abraham are able to understand his teaching about the unending separation of good from bad, once life here is completed, at the Final Judgment, and life thereafter.

Abraham offers a first reason for not helping the rich man. The rich man received his good things in his life on earth; Lazarus received bad things. Now the rich man suffers and Lazarus is consoled. The roles are reversed. The point of Abraham's saying is to give reason why the rich man's suffering will not be interrupted: living in torment as he does now, he should remember that he did have good things in his life on earth and that he is to suffer now. Lazarus, on the other hand, should not be made to abandon his state of happiness; he had suffering all his life, and is now being consoled.

To repeat: Lazarus is not to help the rich man because Lazarus is being consoled and should not interrupt this state to help the rich man. Moreover, the rich man suffers for his sins and Lazarus is not allowed to change that. We recall again that Abraham's statement about the two lots, of the rich man and of Lazarus, means only to explain one thing: not why each man is where he is, but why Lazarus cannot be asked to aid the rich man.

Abraham's explanation has a second part. As mentioned above, in the concept of Hades as described in the parable, there is a chasm, apparently to be imagined as in some sense physical, between good and bad which cannot be breached; no one can cross this chasm. Note that the chasm is "between you and us", a statement in which Abraham includes himself. The chasm is implacably fixed by Another, not by any creature.

One can see that the additional reason why Lazarus cannot help the rich man — no one can cross the chasm that exists between the rich man and Lazarus — is the better explanation of the situation. The text shows this, when Abraham begins his second argument against help for the rich man — it begins with "and on top of this", as though to say that, even if Abraham might think to send Lazarus to help the rich man in the name of mercy, he cannot, for, whether one agrees he should help or not, there is a sure chasm which simply cannot be crossed. And this impossibility ends any discussion of Lazarus bringing help to the rich man.

B. *The second half of the dialogue (vv. 27-31)*

The rich man turns his attention from himself to his five brothers. We are not concerned now about alleviating the suffering of the rich man. He no longer thinks of his own need, but of his five brothers: he wants to keep them from undergoing the suffering that he must bear. The way to achieve this, the rich man thinks, is to send Lazarus to warn the brothers of the frightening danger which lies ahead of them. One might rightly recall the physical nearness or proximity of families; perhaps these brothers had actually lived with him in the same family home - the rich man then would know the state of his brothers, that they needed guidance.

Abraham counters this suggestion of the rich man with a solution of his own. The brothers already know how to avoid the sufferings now being experienced by the rich man: let them listen to Moses and the prophets. Now it is clearer why the rich man is suffering; he has not listened to Moses and the prophets — in Luke, the real meaning of 'listening' is 'obeying' and 'not to listen' is to 'disobey'. Everything becomes fully clear when we put into play the fundamental moral law of Israel: love of God and love of neighbor. Now one is able to interpret most clearly the picture Jesus drew in the first four verses of the parable: the rich man, in doing nothing to care for the blind Lazarus, did not listen to Moses and the prophets, and so must come to his present suffering.

The rich man does not deny the correctness of Abraham's statement: one must love God and love neighbor. But the rich man thinks that they will listen best if someone, in this case Lazarus, should return from the dead to deliver the prophetic, Mosaic message. It is not that Lazarus will have more to say than did Moses; Lazarus's value lies in his knowledge of the world of Hades and to what he can give personal witness. One can talk about the future world, but to hear that world described by someone who has actually been there — that should be convincing.

The reply of Abraham is quite a commentary on the human heart. If one is unwilling to obey Moses and the prophets, no one rising from the dead will move him to obey. So deeply rooted in people must be the refusal to repent that not even the spectacular vision of the dead come to life to describe the sufferings consequent upon disobedience — not even that vision will move one to repentance. Abraham's analysis of a human being in sin is authoritative: the parable intends it to be; that is why the parable ends with his observation. One might think him wrong, but his judgment is not to be challenged: so difficult is repentance of the human heart!

There is no further discussion between Abraham and the rich man; there is no further suggestion that could solve the problem facing the five brothers than that given by Abraham. They have the means to avoid suffering: they must listen to (obey) Moses and the prophets. There being no further suggestion to make, Jesus ends his parable there. So what did love of wealth, while scorning the needy, achieve?

A final consideration has to do with the 'one who rises from the dead'. Some scholars think that Luke, looking back on the fifty or so years since Jesus gave this parable, means to imply (at least imply) that people will not listen to the risen Jesus; Luke's Acts, among other New Testament writings, show proofs, over years, of this 'not listening'. Indeed, some ancient manuscripts have changed the Greek word for 'rising from the dead' so as to more easily make one think of Jesus raised from death; they insert a word commonly used to speak of Jesus risen. Thus, they suggest, though Jesus' final word in the parable speaks about the risen Lazarus or someone like him, Luke would prefer to understand here that it is Jesus who will not be obeyed. The parable has power without reference to Jesus, but it undoubtedly also has power with reference to him. The question is undecided.

13. Useless Servants (Luke 17, 7-9 [10])

A parable?

These verses of Luke are often cited as forming a 'parable'. This claim is justified because it is based on a fictitious statement of an imagined meeting between a master and his field servants, which statement has relevance for the religious world. While Jesus story is fictitious, it does reflect the master-servant relationship of Jesus' world; Jesus' audience understood very well (though some might bristle at the image) the expectations of the master in regard to his servant, just as Jesus presented it.

The parable — an appeal to the audience

With the formula he chooses to introduce this parable, Jesus engages the audience immediately; it calls on them to make a judgment (a fine technique for preaching, and often used by Jesus). They have had the kind of experience Jesus describes — all too often they have been on the 'servant' end of the picture — and so can answer the question for themselves. At the same time, however, we can rightly suggest that the story, while a direct appeal to his hearers, is meant by Jesus to lead up to the answer he himself gives (v. 10) to his own opening question.

Servants — and their masters

However one feels about masters and servants, the reality in the first century (and not only then) was the division of classes, masters and servants. Most field workers who were servants of a master lived in a village and came out to work for the master, then returned to their village with a small sum of money for their labor, to find their own lodging and food. Sometimes, these people would wait in a public place in their village in hope that a master would pass by and hire them, a hiring that could take place at most any time of the day, according to the needs of the master. This was a daily anxiety, for from their field work they and their families survived. Another kind of servant or worker is the one who lived in the house, or on the estate of a master. He, or she, had the security of the estate and potentially a certain degree of familiarity with the family of the master. Their sustenance came from the larders and shelves of the master's kitchen; usually this kind of servant received no wage. In either case, field worker or house servant, the superiority of the master was clear, as was the indebtedness of the servant. The relationship between master and servant was very clear: the more important person, the master, was always the one served. The picture Jesus uses here represents something of an exception in one detail: we have here a field worker who does not live in the village in the evening, but rather returns to quarters on the estate of the master. In a moment we will see another, and striking, exceptional detail.

Judge this!

Jesus describes to us what are likely words a master would address to his servant as he finishes his day's work in the field, whether it be ploughing or sheepherding. Jesus points to the moment when the fatigue of the servant meets the dinner hour of the master. While Jesus counts on his audience's sympathetic awareness of the servant's tiredness, he asks whether that lack of energy will require that the master take care of the servant before his own meal needs are met.

The words of the master reflect the state of servanthood in Israel, but the fact of it made the master's words, if not agreeable, understandable. Given this social gradation in society, the words of the master ring true: it is more reasonable that the master be served by the servant, no matter how tired and ready for dinner he may be, than that the master urge the returning servant to sit right down to his own meal.

Is that not the way things are supposed to happen? asks Jesus. First the servant fulfils all his duties to please his master, and then he can enjoy himself.

Conclusion

Jesus immediately and briefly draws the right conclusion from his fictitious story. His audience, he indicates, is in the role of the servant with regard to God who is Master: 'You are servants'. Under this title of Master, we consider for a moment the early picture of Israel and God. The Sinai covenant and its traditions have ruled the lives of Israelites into Jesus' own generation. The word 'covenant' means to represent the union of two individuals, often of unequal standing the one to the other. The covenant of Sinai portrays the God-Israel relationship as that of King to vassal or servant. In this union, each promises to the other what each can give (indeed, marriage is another way of expressing this 'giving to the other all that I can give'). The Sinai covenant shows God as giving both His wisdom and His promise of protection, which is a promise of His power; this should assure the happiness of the covenant partner. The vassal, Israel, promises all it can give: to God, who has everything, Israel gives obedience, and fully.

Jesus' audience is reminded of this centuries' old relationship with Yahweh, when Jesus recalls that 'you are servants'. He goes further to underline the 'doing' of Israel: our moral acts are simply the concrete expressions of our obedience as servants to our Master.

When all is said and done, with this parable Jesus wishes to underline the one reality, that obedience is owed to God; being a covenant partner with God is a gift, obedience to God is not. This is because 'we are His servants', which has been the understanding in Israel since God said, "I will be your God, and you will be My people". This understanding of reality underlies Jesus' mission in life to call people back to God, to urge them to obey the Law of God, who, of course, will provide all He can for the happiness of Israel. Indeed, there is no other God but Yahweh, and so there is no other source of fullest happiness except Yahweh.

Context

Luke has placed this parable at the end of a few originally disparate sayings (vv. 1-6). Experts have tried, without complete satisfaction, to show the logical unity that joins these sayings together. Nonetheless, it is the fact that our parable, which begins with Jesus' question in v. 7, must somehow be related first at least to v. 6, for Jesus' question follows upon v. 6 with no pause or any kind of introduction.

What we have in vv. 5-6 looks to faith. The disciples ask for faith, with their question suggesting that they have some faith. Jesus seems to suggest that indeed they have less faith than they think; they do not even have faith the size of one seed of the mustard plant, the smallest of seeds. The reason they had asked Jesus for an increase of faith is that his preceding teaching (forgive the one asking for forgiveness, no matter how often he asks) is very difficult. An increase of faith will help them obey. Jesus does not deny the value of increased faith, but he does doubt that they have enough faith to carry out the obedience they owe to God, their Master and covenant partner.

This complaint of Jesus about the faith of his disciples suggests a link with our parable. Recognizing the misunderstanding of the disciples, that they had faith, just not enough faith to obey always, Jesus takes advantage of this notion of obedience and offers a parable that sets straight the status of the disciples: they are servants. It means little, in a certain sense, that the servant finds it difficult to carry out all his orders. But it is clear what his obligations are to his master, even in difficult situations. The master-servant reality is a good example of setting religious reality straight: the servant should act like a servant. The disciples are deserving of this criticism about the paucity of their faith but, through the parable, are asked to look on themselves for what they truly are: servants who owe obedience to Yahweh. The teachings of Jesus which precede vv. 5-6 are hard teachings and demand trust in Jesus' wisdom and obedience through him to God. Should one think of himself as having faith, yet not obey the teachings of Jesus? Rather, we are to listen to Jesus as servants, no matter the difficulties of his commands. In this way, the parable finds a link with what has preceded it: the teaching is hard (do nothing to weaken your neighbour's faith by being unforgiving), but it is the will of the Lord, and we, his servants, know our role and obey.

Note

In translations, Jesus asks his listeners to think of themselves as 'useless' servants. The translation 'useless' seems erroneous. First, the servant of the parable can hardly be called useless: he has worked usefully in the fields all day. Second, in our obedience to God, God never calls us 'useless'; at least there is no record of that in the Scriptures. Third, the Greek word, which many translate as 'useless', is quite rare and so examples are lacking from Greek literature in general by which to establish its true meaning. From the make-up of the Greek word and the context of the parable Jesus uses to teach, it seems best to understand 'useless servant' to point to that servant who has no right to ask for any other treatment that what his reality allows him to claim. Thus, the believer in Jesus and God is urged, in a negative way, to define himself according to his relationship with God as spelled out at Mt. Sinai: he is servant of God and obedient to Him, no matter how difficult God's teachings are. He is nothing else than servant, and glorious only for that. He is not useless, but he is always servant and, in relation to the divine commands, no more.

14. THE JUDGE AND THE WIDOW (LUKE 18, 2-5 [1-8])

This parable, colourful because of its feisty widow squared off before a haughty judge, offers more than one meaning to Luke's readers. The reason for this is that there seems to be in play two different situations. On the one hand, the judge of the story suggests a teaching about God, as the antithesis of this judge: unlike the judge, God will be just, He will hear the plea of the needy. On the other hand, the woman of the story suggests perseverance in prayer. These two possible emphases end with an anxious question, "When the Son of Man comes, will he find that the faith has endured?"

We pay attention to the parable itself, first, but then also to the influences of Luke's introduction to it and Jesus' final words about the Son of Man.

The scene

The legal system in Jesus' day has a part to play in the New Testament. Whether one thinks of the trials before Sanhedrin and Roman authority in the Gospels or of appearances of Apostles before Jewish and Roman tribunals in Acts, the Scriptures keep us aware of circumstances which lead to legal and judicial confrontations. Christianity found it hard to avoid all arraignment before lawful authorities, who were forced to judge the rightness or wrongness, the legality of Christianity.

The parable Jesus now offers, though involving the Jewish legal authority, has little detail about legal matters in it. As usual with parables, the material is reduced to what is necessary to make the point. In this case, we do not know at all any specifics of the widow's complaint; we only know that she wanted justice against her adversary (whoever that might be). Some suggest that, because only certain causes, e.g. financial justice, needed just one judge, the widow's complaint had to do with money. But our attention is directed, not to this point nor to the legal system, but to the mindsets of the two people involved, judge and widow.

The judge is the first to be introduced; as is usual, we are to know about him only what matters to Jesus. Remarkably he is described rather bluntly, and there is no room for lessening the harsh description of him: he has neither fear of God nor respect for human beings. A Jewish audience could not miss the impact of this description: every Israelite was called upon to love God wholeheartedly and love neighbor as oneself; on the other hand, the tradition embedded in the Psalms makes clear the existence and problem of unjust judges. There is no indication that any other legal person is involved than a Jew (though probably a low-level magistrate); his character, judged in the light of the Old Testament, is quickly known to be evil. There is no reason to think, either, that Jesus' audience would balk at the idea of a judge of this bad a character; no surprise here!

Then we are introduced to the other person of the parable, a widow. We know nothing else about this woman, not even her age or income or degree of dependence or her adversary. Apparently Jesus means to focus just upon her widowhood, and let the long traditions of mercy toward the needy widow be uppermost in the minds of his listeners. 'Widows' made up one of the three elements in the venerable, classic group of oppressed: the widow, the orphan and the resident immigrant in Israel. All the audience's pity should be toward this woman; it is particularly upsetting to hear that she encounters a judge who 'has no respect for human beings'. That widows were often poorly treated is well known in the writings of many peoples of the first century AD; was it not the poor treatment of the widows that led in Acts 6 to the creation of deacons in the Jewish Christian community?

The widow thinks she has a just cause here, and there is nothing in the parable to suggest her cause was unjust; the widow has all sympathy, and the love owed to one in need. The widow shows a second characteristic: she is persistent. She is persistent to the point that the unfeeling and uncaring judge in charge of her case is finally moved to act. Indeed, such is her presence before him that he is afraid of a possible black eye (the basic meaning of the Greek verb Jesus uses) from the woman.

There are three sources of meaning for the parable: the parable itself, and as mentioned, the first verse of chapter 18 and vv. 6-8a. We look at them in that order.

The meaning of the parable taken by itself (vv. 2-5)

The parable itself, which runs from v. 2 through v. 5, is very brief. One can argue, within these parameters of the parable alone, which is the principal character of the parable. Certainly much direct address (v. 4-5), a literary sign of the importance of a character and of his opinion, belongs to the judge; perhaps it is in him that the parable's lesson is taught? The widow, too, has a few words in literary direct address; should she be considered the central character of the parable? Should we study her?

Strictly speaking, nothing can be deduced from the parable itself; there is no apparent, clear lesson in it — or at best, there are two lessons, one drawn from the judge ('do not be unjust'), the other from the widow ('persevere in your request'). In this situation, we can best conclude that what we have here is to serve as the basis for a teaching, but a teaching which must be expressed by Jesus or Luke; the parable, by itself, needs help to teach the Gospel lesson.

The parable in the light of introductory verse 1

Luke introduces the parable about the judge and the widow by a reference to prayer. In an earlier moment (Luke 11, 1-13) Jesus, at the request of his disciples, taught them the Our Father as a significant content of prayer, and he emphasized the willingness of God to respond to His children; they are to look upon him as more willing to accept their prayer than is a human father when he hears the requests of his children. In Luke 11 we can say that attention focuses on the prayer of petition, which includes even the petition for forgiveness; what is not addressed here is formal and sacrificial Temple public prayer or liturgy. Here the teaching is on the level of personal prayer.

In the verse which introduces our parable, however, the precise focus is not on trust in God's response to prayer (perhaps it is assumed?), but on the continuousness of prayer and, conversely, that one never tire of prayer. We are not sure, from this introductory verse, if there is any particular type of prayer intended here, but the immediately preceding context suggests perhaps that it is the prayer for readiness to pass the Final Judgment that Luke has in mind.

The background of the parable leading to verse 1

Luke 17, 20-37 (which complete chapter 17) is what comes to Jesus' mind as a suitable response to the question, "When will the kingdom of God come?"; his remarks end with another question, "Where, Lord, will this kingdom come?". In between these anxious and perennial questions are a number of observations that suggest readiness for the coming of the Kingdom, whenever and wherever that is. In the light of this discussion about the eschatological coming of the Judge, one is led to believe that the subject Jesus turns to next — pray continually and do not tire — is prayer which is concerned with readiness for the Final Coming.

Is this eschatological context, a speech which precedes our parable, the only sign that the prayer the parable serves to encourage is concerned with the coming of the Kingdom? No, actually Jesus is preoccupied after the parable (18, 8b) with the same event: the coming of the Son of Man is the moment of judgment of all peoples at the end of this age (or 'eschaton'). Thus, the context which leads into the parable and the content that leads away from it suggests that the continued prayer Jesus urges is the prayer to be saved at the Last Judgment.

As mentioned earlier, while the prayer about the Final Judgment may be the prayer about which Luke is concerned in his introductory verse 1, we will soon see another piece of context, namely verses 7 and 8a, which offer another motive for continued prayer.

In any event, there is no convincing argument (such as context) from Luke's presentation in vv. 1-8 that he is thinking of any and every kind of persevering prayer, e.g. for health, good fortune, wisdom. It is not that he does not urge continued prayer in these and all other matters; indeed, such prayer can fall under Jesus' words that we "ask and seek and knock," since God is an all-powerful and all-loving Father who is concerned for us always and everywhere, and it is through prayer that "he who asks, receives, and he who seeks, finds, and he who knocks, has the door opened for him" (Luke 11, 9-13).

Once one takes into account the command (v. 1) which introduces the parable (which command itself concludes the context of c. 17 before it), we can look to our parable and draw a positive content of prayer from a concrete, fictitious story. It is the widow's insistent requests that help explain her winning justice from the heartless judge; she is an example of one who 'prays continually and does not tire' in her effort to succeed. Again, an introductory verse helps us make sense of the parable — and here a parable concretizes in bold example the fruit of continued prayer. Implicitly then, the thinking goes: if widow could win justice by virtue of continued prayer, we can win salvation at the Final Judgment through continued prayer. In this view, it seems that the widow is the person who expresses the main point of the parable.

The parable in the light of Jesus' words in the concluding verses 6 - 8a

The first words of Jesus, offering meaning to the parable, can be put in a question form of two types. First, his question is adamant: "Could you ever imagine for a moment that God would not do justice for his elect who pray to Him day and night?" Then his question (as presented in the Greek text) is less passionate: "Do you think He would delay in their regard?" Jesus leaves no time for a response from his audience to this twofold question; he already knows the answer, as does his audience. The implied answer is that "He will surely not refuse His help to His chosen ones, and He will surely not delay".

But Jesus does not leave the answer implied. He wants to underline most explicitly and clearly what the reaction of God to prayer will be: "I assure you, God will certainly give justice to His elect, and swiftly". Jesus' answer to his own twofold question is firm, confident, even challenging: how could it be otherwise, given who God is and who His elect are?

Helping Jesus make his point about the swiftness of God's merciful reply is the presentation of an anti-figure like the judge: one who has no sympathy for the widow and no respect for God (and so does not hold himself obliged to obey the supreme law: 'You shall love God, your neighbor as yourself'). If someone like him could finally give a positive response, how much more will God the Father, the opposite of this unjust figure, give a positive response! To the lesson taught through the figure of the judge, then, the figure of the widow adds her own encouragement to those who might waver in prayer: she is presented as thoroughly persevering. How like the widow are Christians persecuted for their faith! And so, by the contrast Jesus offers in the interplay between these two figures of judge and widow, he leads the audience to agree that there really is no reason why persistent prayer to an all-good and all-loving and all-powerful God should long go unheard. If understanding the true nature of God is the point of the parable, then it seems that the unjust judge is the central character of the parable.

One is tempted to recall that God has already been presented in the Gospel as Father, and so one might bring to the interpretation of the parable this meaning of God, so as to make Jesus' affirmation (certainly He will not delay!) all the more convincing. But Luke has not used this word 'Father'. He has used another word 'the elect' to explain God's faithfulness to those who pray night and day. 'Elect' has a long history in the Jewish Scriptures, where it means those who have been chosen, set apart by the love of God; it also appears, very significantly, in many texts having to do with persecution. Its sense of 'being chosen apart from others' (and so often violently estranged from others) is very much a part of the circumstance of the word in Jewish persecution tradition (as well as elsewhere in the New Testament, particularly, again, in times of persecution). Also, the word itself, 'elect', bears the sense of the passive voice: a person chosen, elected by someone. Thus the choice is not that of the chosen one, but of Him who, for His own reasons, chooses. The motive for this divine choice is love, and this love is necessarily defined, in the case of God, to be both unconditional and free from any constraint. It is to these whom He has chosen, or separated from others, that He will respond and not delay.

Though the language be different, in the long run we have here teaching that mirrors what Jesus had already taught (and we have already mentioned): 'If your father who is evil knows how to give you good things, how will God who loves you deny you the best, even His own Holy Spirit?' (Luke 11, 13).

Background of the parable in light of verses 6-8a

But our parable at chapter 18 is not simply a repetition of what Jesus had said at Luke 11, 13, which has to do with prayer about a variety of matters; vv. 6-8a seem concentrated on a particular and significant background. We have already suggested that the background to this parable indicates that Luke at v. 1 is concerned that one prays continually to be able to pass the Final Judgment. Now, in light of vv. 7-8a and its language of election (which signals persecution), together with the clear emphasis in the parable on justice-injustice, it seems reasonable to think that the background of Jesus' teaching here is persecution, possibly of various sorts, of the followers of Jesus, of the chosen. Certainly, this parable, with this understanding, is useful for the times of persecution of the later Christian communities and missionaries Luke will describe in the Acts of the Apostles. In identifying a persecution-background for Jesus' teaching here, we do not mean to undercut the earlier interpretation of the parable: preparation for passing the Final Judgment. Indeed, neither background contradicts the other, but can be seen as both having a part in better understanding the parable; both backgrounds lead to valuable teachings drawn from the parable.

Jesus' concluding observation

Verse 8b turns from the positive and cheering note of vv. 6-8a by suggesting the possibility that the Son of Man may not find 'the faith' when he returns in Judgment. As noted earlier, this verse 8b brings our attention to the problem of passing the Final Judgment. Describing Jesus as Son of Man means to indicate the Jesus who will judge mankind at the end of time. Can we be sure that the Judge will find 'this faith' on earth? This verse adds a certain soberness when one considers the readiness of a follower of Jesus to pass the Last Judgment.

Verse 8b asks whether or not Jesus will find 'the faith' when he returns as Judge of the world; he speaks about 'the faith', the Greek indicates, and not simply 'faith'. The faith involved here most likely has the specific content that has Jesus at its center with his teachings. Thus, Jesus asks, will the Son of Man upon his return find faith in me and my teachings? But there is another characteristic of 'the faith' which, while not excluding what we have already said, focuses more directly on the problem which moves Luke's use of our parable. And what is 'this faith'? It is the faith that underlies continued prayer, and without which prayer will not be continued and one will grow tired. That is, the faith in question here is specific: the belief that God will surely hear our prayers and will come to us swiftly.

The problem with Luke 18, 1-8

We have a particular and nagging problem in our story of 18, 1-8. It begins simply in the fact that the introductory verse 1 speaks only of continued, untiring prayer; it does not speak of a swift response to prayer. Verses 6-8a, on the contrary, have at their heart the claim that God will hear prayer and respond swiftly. One might compare this contrast among verses with the two backgrounds we have suggested: one prays untiringly to be saved at the end of time without any knowledge when this end might come, and so without expecting God to come swiftly, but one prays in immediate persecutions for a swift end to them.

Added to the contrast between v. 1 and vv. 6-8a is the fact that in v. 1 concentration is on the one praying, whereas in vv. 6-8a concentration is on the reality of God who hears prayer.

We can presume that when Luke wrote vv. 1-8a he was aware of the contrasts we have noted and let them let stand. That is, on the one hand he wanted his reader to persevere in prayer and not tire of it, whenever it may be answered, and on the other hand never wants to doubt that God cannot but hear His elect and answer them swiftly. The parable of Jesus about the judge and the widow help explain these two desired teachings: on the one hand, continued prayer is answered, and on the other hand, God, quite the opposite of an unjust judge — who would ever accuse Him of delay? But Luke also feels he must include the final word of Jesus: will the disciple really continue to believe unflaggingly that God so loves His people that He cannot do anything but respond to their prayer, and swiftly?

It is helpful to think that the contrast between untiring prayer and prayer swiftly answered is owed to two different situations: one, the long wait for the Final Judgment; the other, the quick end to a particular persecution. To the latter God will act swiftly; to the former, who knows when the Son of Man will bring an end to this world and so bring persevering prayer to its conclusion? But whatever one decides about the influence of the situations which gave rise to the statements in v. 1 and in vv. 6-8a, one is still left with the intention of Luke: pray untiringly, with confidence that God's response will be guided only by love. Trust that He will act swiftly. But, turning from what is expected from God to what is expected of the elect, we hear Jesus' words in 8b: will the Son of Man, upon his return to earth, find this faith in God, this knowledge of God, still alive and burning, still strong enough to sustain and drive continual prayer?

Conclusion

Our parable has prayer as its subject, as v.1 so clearly indicates, but, by the end of Jesus' remarks on the occasion served by the parable, it is clear that what is at stake is one's estimate of the love of God for the one praying and one's own faith in this love. So often it comes down to this: do I really believe in His love for me? Jesus was faced with this challenge, too; he thought the better thing for his good was to avoid death. It is only his confidence in his Father's love for him that made him say, every time he said he did not want to die, "Your will, not mine, be done". Ultimately, here as in every other circumstance of his life, he let the knowledge of his Father's love for him guide his decisions and actions. He is occasionally recorded as having spent the night in prayer, which suggests that there were still many other, shorter times of prayer. His continued prayer shows his own faith in the love of his Father for him; he becomes a model to answer Luke's concern, pray always and do not tire. His one recommendation to his disciples when in the Garden was to get up and pray (22, 46). And indeed God always found Jesus persevering in prayer (consider his words to his Father on the cross), to the time when God finally came to take him to Himself.

A final look at our parable. In short, if an unjust and uncaring judge can, out of a kind of self-preservation, finally dispense justice, what will a loving Father do? Will His love make Him delay, or make Him act swiftly? The widow won her justice by continued harassment of a boorish judge; in light of her situation, what can be said about constant prayer to God? Can we doubt that a prayer which needs perseverance will not be efficacious on our behalf? Why doubt?

(The words about God's 'coming swiftly' make up one of the difficult texts regarding the time of the end of this world, the time of Judgement. Admittedly, Luke has given up trying to identify this time, though he will not omit such texts as we have before us. Luke has written his overall work on the supposition that the Kingdom may come only after a long time has passed; why then speak of it as 'coming swiftly'? Indeed, a difficult question, if not impossible to answer. Luke has no answer.)

15. The Pharisee and the Publican (Luke 18, 10-13 [9-14])

The actual parable Jesus offers covers vv. 10-13. Verses 9 and 14 are an introduction from Luke and a conclusion from Jesus. The parable depicts an imaginary scene, but to Jesus' audience the scene is all too real. To understand what the audience understands, we should look for a moment at these three elements of the parable — the Temple, the Pharisee and the Tax Collector.

The temple

The one term Temple refers to two things. First, since Jerusalem is built on a mountain top (actually it is built on a mountain with four tops), King Solomon, in order to build a place of worship for Yahweh, had to level off a top of the mountain so that he could build a flat platform on which he could have Israel gather for religious services. This flat platform can be imagined to be about trapezoidal in shape, with each of the walls running north-south about 450-500 yards long. On it will be a number of buildings, each contributing its part to the proper worship of God. This flat platform is called the Temple.

Second, one of the buildings on the Temple platform, the central building, is constructed to resemble a palace. This palace runs west to east, with the 'front door' at the east end (since God was often poetically imagined by Israel to come, like the brilliant and glorious sun, from the East). The back of this palace abuts the western wall of the platform or Temple. This palace is made up of three rooms or areas. There are two enclosed courtyards (at the eastern end of the building) where the women and men of Israel stand to worship God. Then there is a middle room, called The Holy, where we find the altar of incense (this is where Zachary was when Gabriel announced to him that he would have a son) and the perpetually-lit candelabra; into the room itself are allowed only priests, whereas into the two corridors along on either side of this room men of Israel could enter. Finally, there was the western-most room, The Holy of Holies, considered for centuries to be the Dwelling of God on earth, or of His Name or of His Glory; no one entered this room, this house, except the High Priest, and he entered only once a year. This palace, this building of three royal sections, is called the Temple. In front of this Temple, and on the Temple platform, stood the altar on which sacrifices were offered, and a huge basin of water. (The killing of animals, like their selling, took place elsewhere on the Temple platform.)

In the light of the two meanings of the term 'Temple', Jesus means that the Pharisee, a man dedicated to a holy life, certainly was in the first or eastern sector where the men of Israel would be in prayer; he most likely is not in either of the two corridors that run along the sides of the room of the Holy. His prayer is directed to God in Heaven who resides in mysterious form in the Holy of Holies. Jesus probably means the tax collector is also in the place where the men of Israel prayed together, in a position which the Pharisee could see and comment on in his prayer.

The Pharisee does know that the tax collector is in the Temple area, but it is not clear that that means the tax collector is physically close to the Pharisee; probably the Pharisee is referring in his prayer to a figure quite some distance away from his own place of prayer — as would befit a sinner.

The Pharisee

'Pharisee' means one who is 'separate'; fundamentally, what the Pharisee is separate from is sin, or disobedience to the Law of Moses and its authoritative subsequent traditions. The Pharisee group originated as a religious entity opposed to the secularization of the People of Israel, about 180 BC. There were never more than 8000 Pharisees at one time in Palestine; at times members of their group suffered martyrdom for their beliefs. Perhaps not unexpectedly, by the time of Jesus these religious zealots were greatly admired by the general public for their intense devotion to Yahweh, something the ordinary person did not have, and those whose entire lives were lived single-mindedly for Yahweh were strongly critical of those not so devoted; it is easy enough to imagine both an occasional sinful pride in the hearts and actions of some Pharisees and a contempt for those other Jews unwilling to keep the Law of Moses. St. Paul was for years a Pharisee, which to some degree psychologically explains the intensity and single-mindedness of his life to Jesus. That the imagined Pharisee of Jesus' parable did all the things he said in his prayer is not at all unlikely; to say more, fasting more than a few times a year was not obligatory, but an expression of his devotion. (One tenet shared by Pharisee and Christian in the First Century AD was belief in the resurrection of the dead — which Sadducees denied).

The tax collector

The Roman State demanded three things from its conquered territories: men for the Roman army, money (taxes) and peace. To collect its money through taxation, Rome would ordinarily sell the debt to a wealthy person, who, in turn, was allowed to collect from a conquered territory what he had spent in buying the debt from Rome, and then add a percentage for his work. Obviously, in Palestine this one man could not collect all the taxes himself, so he hired tax collectors to collect from the people both the taxes and their own salaries. But these tax collectors could not handle all the work so they became chief tax collectors who would hire many tax collectors to collect the taxes and the salaries of the chief tax collectors, and their own salaries. Thus, to make up an example, Rome may have asked $1,000,000.00 from Palestine in taxes; a rich man would give Rome the $1,000,000.00 and then set about recouping from Palestine his one million, plus his own salary, perhaps $100,000.00. The rich man would hire, let us say, 10 chief tax collectors, each of which would earn $30,000.00, and each of these would hire perhaps 5 tax collectors, each of whom would receive $10,000.00 for his work. These 10 tax collectors would expect there be collected $1,000,000.00 for Rome, plus $100,000.00 for the rich man, plus their own salaries (in our example that would be 10 x $30,000.00 or $300,000.00). The total of money to be gathered now is $1, 400,000.00. Who would collect this money? The fifty minor tax collectors would be included here, at a cost of $500,000.00. So, what had been a taxation by Rome of $1,000,000.00 is now a bill, to be paid by the people, which totals $1,900,000.00! It is estimated that, in the time of Jesus, 50% of one's salary went to pay taxes. Add to this that, in the time of Jesus, tax collectors were known to be so corrupt and untrustworthy in their demands that automatically they could give no witness in a trial! Thus, one can perceive a 'certain history' behind the brief dialogue between the tax collectors and John the Baptist: "What should we do (in repentance)?" "Do not exact more than what is the legitimate limit set for you" (Luke 3, 12). In short, for their indisputable injustices tax collectors (like Matthew) were a despised people. This is our tax collector now who asks for mercy.

The center of the parable — two prayers

A. *The Pharisee's prayer*

In his parable, Jesus pits the quintessential zealot for the will of God against the inexcusably sinful and hated tax collector. Whatever the circumstances surrounding their visit to the Jerusalem Temple, we find them in prayer. The words of the Pharisee are words about himself: he has done many laudable things. Indeed, one might pause at the Pharisee's thanks to God that he is 'not like other Jews, certainly not like this tax collector', but one cannot deny that indeed he is, in his devotional acts, quite different from the many Jews who honor God much less than he. It is quite possible to read in certain psalms of David references to David's good deeds; he does not hesitate to tell God what good he has done, so why should the Pharisee not speak to God similarly?

How are we to evaluate this prayer and the Pharisee who prays in this way? Yes, one can draw parallels between this prayer and the holy prayers of David, but the criterion to determine the value of the Pharisee' prayer does not lie there.

The Pharisee's prayer is to be understood according to the verse (9) which Luke uses to introduce the story to us. There is no use of the title Pharisee here; rather two attitudes are revealed. First, these people have great confidence in their being just before God; they judge their actions and find their lives pleasing to God. Secondly, at the same time they despise all other Jews — clearly for their failures before God. Unsaid, but implied is that the Pharisee can be grateful that he is not like all other Jews. Now we have a key as to how to understand correctly the thanks the Pharisee gives that he is not like others, especially not like this tax collector. Luke's introduction finds no fault in noble deeds done to honor God, to fulfil God's Law. But despising others while otherwise obeying God is simply unacceptable. In the light of this evaluation, one can only judge further, that misplaced is the 'confidence in themselves' that they are holy before God. The attitude of the Pharisee turns out to be the Pharisee's condemnation; he cannot call himself just while despising others! There will come to our notice one other element that is lacking in the prayer of the Pharisee, his lack of awareness of his own sinfulness and his need for forgiveness. He has raised himself up, and fails to see his humiliated state.

B. *The tax collector's prayer*

The introductory verse (9) of Luke does not mention the sinner, the tax collector. This means that Luke, as he enters into the parable, has his sights only on the Pharisee. Why then does he include the prayer of the tax collector?

A first reason is that the prayer helps interpret the Pharisee. The prayer is an expression of humility which is at notable odds with the words of the Pharisee, who, one realizes, admits no faults and asks no pardon. Sadly, there is only one person who admits sin and asks for pardon. In brief, what prayer should not contain, in some way or other, an acute awareness and admission of sin? When one thinks of the Our Father or of the central prayer of the Eucharist, one knows that each contains a very clear statement of the sinfulness of the person praying and of a plea that sins be forgiven. We have here two very different approaches to God and a better understanding of the shortcoming of the Pharisee.

A second reason is to provide the material for the two expressions of Jesus in v. 14. In v. 14a, we have a revelation, which is the Lord's truthful judgment by Jesus about reality as only he knows it; the judgment, the reality has to do with the forgiveness of the sins, both of the imaginary Pharisee and of the imaginary tax collector. The better translation of the Greek says that the Pharisee returns home unforgiven — not that he returns home less forgiven than was the tax- collector. Following this judgment is a proverb (v.14b), without which we would be missing the final clarification of the entire report, vv. 9-14a.

What then is the prayer of the tax collector? It admits sin and requests mercy, compassion. Introducing the listeners to this person is the typically first-century Jewish description of a person seeking pardon: standing at a distance (from the Holy of Holies), he acknowledges physically how far the immoral person feels he should be from the all-holy God; not lifting his eyes to God, because he is not worthy even to look God in the face; beating his breast, because within him is the heart which leads him to sin and which deserves punishment.

C. *What to make of the Pharisee and the tax collector?*

The sinner's body language reinforces the sinner's awareness that he should not even be in the presence of God, and reinforces the logical conclusion of his self-awareness: forgive me! One cannot, in the light of the kind of sin which characterized the tax-collector in Israel, fail to see that his is a sin against Israel's primary covenant law, love of neighbor. There is no indication at all that the sinner thinks that anything he has done would of itself forgive him; maybe he did good deeds, but his final, expressed summation of himself is sinner. That his good deeds do not forgive him is crucial here: he is at the mercy of another, who is free to forgive or not. And on this free act hangs everything, the man's social and religious status in a people called to stand in purity before God and his entrance past the Judgment into the Kingdom of God. His problem: will he find someone who is willing to have mercy on him? He cannot help himself. His self-evaluation is not false; he truly does depend on another to enter eternal happiness. He cannot forgive himself; his only route is to ask someone for mercy — and wait.

Against this picture is that of the Pharisee. In itself his prayer cannot be judged negatively; it is too like prayers of noble people in the Old Testament. But the description with which Luke introduces him is decisive: he is one of those who claim to be just, yet despise the rest of men. The Pharisee's prayer must be evaluated ultimately not in itself, but against the attitude of the Pharisee 'towards all men'. What prayer can be fruitful, if one despises others? Moreover, while the prayer here is one of thanksgiving — and generally speaking this kind of prayer is most praiseworthy — the fact is that it contains no awareness of sin needing forgiveness. Is that bad? It is for a person who despises others, while totalling up his good deeds, particularly for the person who despises and puts this attitude in his prayer: I am so grateful that I am not like others, particularly this tax collector. As mentioned earlier, there is nothing wrong with wanting to be more than a sinner, but vaunting one's gratitude for escaping sin and at the same time lacking in respect and love for those whom "You should love as you love yourself" — this results in unacceptable prayer; it is not prayer that leads to forgiveness of sins.

Another reflection here derives, not from the parable or its surrounding verses (9 and 14), but from the more general context of Jesus' public life: he is after sinners, urging them all day to repent. Given who is telling this parable, it is not hard to see that the Pharisee in no way fits into what Jesus sees as the reality of every life: sin. Looking only at his prayer, one says that the Pharisee is not a sinner. Is that true? Or is Jesus correct in asking even those striving for perfection to realize, too, that they are sinners, and therefore totally dependent for eternal happiness not simply on the good they do, but on the mercy they receive? Without this realization and the subsequent plea for mercy, what good is the prayer of the Pharisee?

Finally, like his prayer, the body language of the Pharisee is revealing. He does raise his eyes, at least to the degree that he can pray about the tax collector 'over there'. He is far from beating his breast and being distant from God: rather he stands, which is a sign of dignity, and he prays about himself in the words which are compromised by his lack of love of neighbor. Good deeds he has done, but woe to him for his failing to love his neighbor!

The reality, which one can say only Jesus knows and reveals, is that the sinner goes home forgiven and the Pharisee not.

It is the quality of humility, in this case the recognition of oneself as sinner and the one man's dire call for mercy that wins him forgiveness, and it is another man's prideful spite of neighbor which wins him no forgiveness at all. If Jesus comes to teach people what is required to enter into the Kingdom of Heaven, humble admission of sins and the plea for forgiveness are central teachings.

Granted, then, that the final sentence of Luke' story is a proverb applicable to many types of situations, it should be said that in the parabolic situation that Luke describes, the entire matter has its complete conclusion only with the proverb. Only with the proverb does one understand fully why the sinner went home forgiven and the Pharisee not. Certainly, one recognizes from Luke's introductory verse the evil of the Pharisee who can praise his admittedly good deeds and at the same time despise others; from that pride we can understand why he remains unforgiven. But the tax-collector? In his case it is his humility which will bring him forgiveness, which will raise him on high. It is the proverb, often used by Jesus and perhaps added here by Luke, which explains most fully the results of the prayers of the Pharisee and tax-collector. One might conclude by thinking: I should know myself and beg forgiveness.

16. PARABLE ABOUT THREE SERVANTS AND THE FINAL JUDGMENT (LUKE 19, 12-27 [11-27])

While they were listening to these things, He went on to tell a parable, because he was near Jerusalem where they thought the reign of God was about to appear" (v. 11). First, this sentence, composed by Luke, means to sum up with the words "these things" the most recent teachings and actions of Jesus that concerned repentance; this perpetual call to repentance becomes all the more insistent as Jesus brings his preaching career to a close. Indeed, a faith which produces the good works of repentance is the meaning of the 'silver which the servants of the king were to increase by trading'. Second, with this sentence Luke calls attention to the fact that Jesus was very near Jerusalem, where many thought he was somehow going to create the Kingdom of God now. (Luke's very next story, which brings to an end Jesus' preaching before Jerusalem, recounts the adulation and ecstasy of the crowds as Jesus comes on a mule [sign of royalty] to Jerusalem — surely this is the crowd's greatest moment in professing Jesus' kingship!)

It will not be surprising then that the parable, in the light of Luke's introductory verse 11, will deal with two points: a king coming to his people, and a repentance which emphasizes living one's faith in obedient actions.

The king

The notion of a king appears twice in this parable, at its opening and at its closing. In the first appearance a wealthy man goes away to be crowned king; we learn immediately upon his departure that he is hated by his fellow citizens to the point that they send a delegation after him to say they do not want him back as their king. In the second appearance, the wealthy man-made-king, upon his return, did what kings traditionally did in this first-century world to their enemies: all his enemies are slaughtered before his eyes. Why speak here of such a king as this? Most all scholars understand Jesus to refer to himself, that is, to his going away to be crowned king (at his Father's right hand), to his being contemned by many of his fellow citizens who refuse to accept him as their king, and to his punishing his enemies at his return at the end of the world as Judge. How fitting that this parable is placed so near to the days which see the refusal of Jesus as king by so many and to Jesus' departure to a 'faraway land'.

We should underline that this story is a particularly apt introduction to the tragedy and glory which begin with the next story (known as Palm Sunday), the praise of Jesus as king — and the subsequent account, in Gospel and Acts, of the contradictory refusal of so many audiences, of the preaching that calls for faith in the crucified Jesus who, as the missionaries will insist, is Israel's king, raised from the dead, and one day Judge.

As the parable opens, and before kingship is mentioned, we are introduced to a well-born and wealthy man. It is this wealthy man who will act throughout the rest of the parable till its last verse. We are to understand that it is this person as king, who, upon his royal return, commands the slaughter of those enemies who did not want him as king, but it is this person as wealthy man who reacts to the success or failure of the money he left for increase.

The parable tells two stories. The first has to do with a deadly antagonism between a new king and the people who did their best that he not be their king. The second has to do with the use of 'money' and its profits. We will talk about both of these aspects of Jesus' parable, but since we mentioned the subject of 'repentance' and since the two aspects of the parable touch on both acceptance of the king and the doing of good deeds, we should note the double form that repentance takes, especially and most directly and clearly in the early preaching of the Acts of the Apostles. There repentance means both a turning to accepting Jesus as Messiah and Lord and a faithful living out of the moral acts Jesus has taught, notably in the Gospel. It is the linking of acceptance of Jesus and fidelity to his teaching that unites the two aspects of Jesus' parable, Jesus' kingship and moral good deeds generated by faith.

The good deeds that flow from true repentance

The way in which the story unfolds emphasizes very clearly that what money was given to the servants is to make more money. (Perplexing is the fact that, while the parable mentions that each of ten servants received a portion of money, actually only the story of three of them is recounted in the parable; some scholars have used this point to say that Luke inherited a story about 'ten', then reduced it to 'three', a 'literary' number which is visible in many of his parables.) The wealthy man will not stand for anything less than profit; not developing his money, then, is most unsatisfactory, almost as bad, one suspects, as losing it would be. Indeed, showing no profit results in losing what one had thought he had saved. "To the man who has, more will be given; and he who has not, will lose even the little he thinks he has" (Luke 8, 18). Such is the teaching of the parable, but to what is Jesus referring when he recounts here fictitious lives of success and failure?

The Story

Jesus' imaginary story no doubt reflects the experiences of the audience of his time. His hearers understand the responsibilities laid upon servants by their masters. In this case, the entire fictitious story focuses on an initial lending of money, the same amount in each servant's case, and the expectation of the wealthy man that he receive a return which shows a profit. The story unfolds as a reasonable example of master-servant relationship. The master clearly wants his money to make money. Thus, a decision to hide the money, so as not to lose it in trading, is not acceptable, no matter what the servant's thinking might be. We hear of the master's distribution of wealth and his commands to make a profit, and we are present at the reckoning about these profits. This moment of reckoning allows us to see reward and punishment. The religious reality this fictitious story reveals has to do with a God-given gift which produces no value. Value (in the story it is money) is the desire of the master; he rewards value and punishes its absence. What religious reality fits this story about 'stewardship meant to produce profit'?

The simplest and traditional answer of the interpreter is that God expects deeds (the equivalent of profit) in accord with the Mosaic Law as taught by Jesus, and will give a reward to each person in some respect commensurate with what he has done in his moral life; thus, having passed the Judgment, one will receive a greater reward, another a lesser reward — according to the moral good he has done on earth.

The problem with this interpretation lies in the question: are we all given the same degree of faith? Certainly, faith is often described simply, without any reference to degree of faith; perhaps that is all that is meant here in the parable: each person received the equivalent of faith and will show the fruits of that faith at the Final Judgment. Certainly it is true that faith, at the end of one's life, can be seen as having produced so much goodness in the life of one person, another amount of good in the life of another.

The entire Gospel as guide

Jesus has defined his public life as a life that calls people to repentance so as to be able to enter the kingdom of God; indeed, Jesus is known for his emphasis on good deeds. The parable of the Good Samaritan underlines 'what I must do to inherit eternal life' — 'go, and do as the Samaritan has done' (10, 25 and 37). "Give to all who beg from you...Do to others as you would have them do to you" (6, 30-31). "Love your enemy and do good" (6, 35). "A good man produces goodness from his heart...Why do you call me 'Lord, Lord', and do not put into practice what I teach you; any man who desires to come to me will hear my words and put them into practice" (6, 45.46.47). "The seed on good ground are those who hear the word in a spirit of openness, retain it, and bear fruit through perseverance" (8, 15). "My mother and my brothers are those who hear the word of God and act on it" (8, 21). "Blessed are they who hear the word of God and keep it" (11, 27). "These are the things you should practice, without omitting the others" (11, 42). "No, when one of you gives a banquet, invite beggars and the crippled, the lame and the blind…you will be repaid in the resurrection of the just" (14, 13-14). Against this repeated insistence, which continues on beyond the life of Jesus to pervade the Acts of the Apostles, one leans toward the interpretation that sees the parable as addressing the fruits (or not) of one's faith. If this be the right interpretation, then the sums of money in the parable smoothes out to become, simply, the faith each person has by which he produces good deeds. That is to say, it would be erroneous, on the basis of the parable, to say that children at baptism receive varying degrees of faith; this conclusion cannot be sustained from anything else said in the New Testament. Surely, God is free to bestow his gift of faith to the degree he wishes, but that is not affirmed as such in the New Testament.

The third servant

We turn now to the third servant and his plight. Here we have no productivity, which is unfortunately the only thing the rich man expected from his servants. Given this clear intention of the master ("Put this money to work," he said, "until I come back" [v. 13], keeping the money safe but showing no profit — this is contrary to the will of the rich man; it is disobedience. The parable tells us the reasoning by which the servant kept safe and unproductive the money he was supposed to trade upon. One might 'understand' a servant who has fears of losing what is not his, but if one is inclined to think that there is a certain reasonableness to this servant's words to his master, he is mistaken. The parable does intend that the audience not sympathize with this third servant; he is supposed to trade, not hide.

What is problematic here is the description of the master that the servant gives; granted that a human master can be described this way, should we say that the parable means to describe the God of the real world in these terms? The question is not useless. That God is exacting or demanding is a reality which one might want to replace with 'merciful' or 'kindly' or 'forgiving', but this runs counter to the general teaching of Jesus, and of the rest of the New Testament. There is no question that Jesus' world is one that includes demands, and reward or punishment. Of course, it is one of the hallmarks of Jesus' perception of God that he raises a human being's awareness of the Creator's love for His creature; like his tradition but even moreso, he emphasizes, beyond human dreams, the intense love of God for human beings, particularly the faithful, and the New Testament follows suit. But this revelation does not coerce Jesus to deny that God is demanding and exacting, now and in the hereafter. However, that the fictitious master is described as one who 'takes up what he did not lay down and harvests what he did not plant' (i.e. profits for himself from another's work) is a fair description for the master of the parable, but does not 'fit' with the understanding of God, for the reason that nowhere in the teaching of Jesus is God described this way, nor does the New Testament suggest that God should be described this way. These words are after the manner of a proverb, drawn from human activities such as harvesting, and applicable to many human situations. They are not, however, directly applicable to God.

What are we to think is the final state of the third servant? Clearly the rich man is disappointed and even angry that this servant did not trade (should we say, 'trade successfully'?) on the money which was entrusted to him to make a profit. Perhaps a reason for the wealthy man's frustration is that he counted on his servants to gain money for him while he was away to receive kingship? The final outcome of the servant is a bit strange. The parable does not say that he was punished (though soon enough, in the case of the wealthy man's return as king, we will hear the subject of violent punishment brought up). What we learn to be the fate of the servant is that he will have the money which was entrusted to him for a profit taken away from him. If the parable does not describe more obvious punishment, are we to assume that the taking back of this money is a form of punishment?

Certainly in the real world of God there is punishment for not performing good deeds. What seems to be part of the message of the parable is that, punishment aside, the servant is no longer to be trusted to make money for his master. This lack of trust seems to be the final conclusion to the servant's inactivity. One wonders if this aspect can be applied to the real world of God, namely that God will not entrust faith to anyone who does not produce good deeds from it. Perhaps, if we want to stay with this possibility, we should say that anyone who does not produce good deeds will lose his faith, and not that God will take it from him. In this sense we can say that the lack of trust in the servant can be translated, in the world of religion, to permission that faith be lost. God is not the cause of this moral evil, but permits it — a principle deduced from the teachings throughout the New Testament. In any event, it is the servant who, by his inactivity, produces no 'profit' or good deed, and so loses the basis for 'profit-making'; that is, he loses his faith.

But this emphasis on 'taking away' serves another purpose in the parable. In the parable what is taken away from the third servant is then bestowed on the servant who made the most profit from his efforts at trading. As the description stands, there seems to be no relation between it and religious life; one person's failure to produce good deeds, since he has lost his faith, does not lead God to give the failed person's faith or its profit to another. This aspect of the parable remains in the world of fiction. On the other hand, this 'taking' and 'giving' does allow Jesus to introduce the proverb, 'to everyone who has, more will be given, and from the one who has nothing, even what he has will be taken away'. As indicated, this total sentence cannot be a principle of religious life if it is applied to the giving of one's person's faith to another, but there can be a restricted application. That is, to one who has good deeds, a reward worth more than the good deeds will be given, and to the one who has lost his faith, his final state will be that of the total loss of faith. These ideas one can find in or deduce from the teaching of Jesus and the New Testament.

The close of the parable

After reading the parable Luke gives us, it seems quite understandable to say that the parable rightly ends with the final words of the rich man about the reward of obedience and the loss incurred by disobedience. But of course it doesn't. To finish off what had been begun, Jesus brings home the rich man, now become king. This element of the parable, which seems 'extra' to the bulk of the parable's three servants (and so, to some scholars, is an addition to the original parable told by

Jesus), is made clearer from an awareness of the Gospel context, when one realizes that Luke has us on the verge of Jesus' ascending to his Father with the expectation that he will return to pass judgment on those who had passed condemnatory judgment on him. With the final order of the rich man-king, those who had been fellow-citizens of the rich man and sent word that "We do not want him ruling us" are put to the sword in the sight of their new king. Again, the terminology is fitting for its day in the first-century Mediterranean world, but there is nothing in the teaching of Jesus or in the rest of the New Testament which describes God's world this way. At times, the Old Testament can approach this extreme brutality, and these parable words might remind us of references to divine destruction in the Old Testament (e.g. Psalm 11, 6) and 2 Peter 2's tirade against sinners, but these latter are not as vicious as are the words that describe the new king come home, who 'slaughters his enemies in his sight'.

Finally, it seems clear to identify Jesus as the master who went away to a far-off place to receive a crown, only to come back to his people for judgment. No doubt most ancient Jewish prophets expected a final judgment of Israel, but they expected it to be carried out by God. Only rarely, e.g. Daniel 7, is there the suggestion that God will hand over the judgment to "another like a son of man'. Jesus picked up on this prophet's image and used it often. Since Jesus has for long identified himself as Son of Man, in his life and in the Gospel, there is no question that the parable has him, and not God, in mind. It is precisely this aspect of judge that moved Jesus to speak of himself as Son of Man, an image which includes a first humiliation of the Son of Man, then his glorification at the right hand of God.

17. THE REBELLIOUS, VICIOUS VINEYARD WORKERS (LUKE 20, 9-16 [17-19])

Where is Jesus' audience?

On the one hand, with this parable we are in Jerusalem, most importantly on the Temple platform and presumably along the inside of its eastern wall. Estimates of the length of the eastern wall center on just over 500 yards. The entire platform or compound serves as a flat surface to smooth off the pointedness of the crests of Mount Zion, is trapezoidal in shape, with the north and south walls each about 60% the length of the east and west walls. Extending westward from this eastern wall is a roof or portico held up by pillars, a roof wide enough to protect visitors from rain and sun. Under this portico one could often find numbers of people gathered to hear a teacher expound his doctrine. So it is here that we find Jesus teaching 'in Jerusalem', and 'in the Temple area'. As Luke tells it (and Mark and Matthew tell it the same way), Jesus came to Jerusalem only at what turned out to be the time of his death; as the Synoptics report, his final approach to the city was greeted with adulation and songs of praise; mistakenly perhaps, but Jesus is thought by the crowds to exercise his role as king here and now. Our parable takes place, then, during one of Jesus' teaching days under the eastern portico of the Jerusalem Temple.

It is here that Jesus encounters a very forceful opponent: the High Priest, Chief Priests (who number about 8) and Scribes (specialists in interpreting the Law of Moses and its traditions); by and large, he had been challenged by Scribes and Pharisees of Galilee; now the main opponent is the Priesthood, located at the religious Center of Israel. It is estimated that the location of the Sanhedrin, the ultimate court of all Israel, where Jesus would soon be tried, is less than about

300 yards or so due west of the eastern portico, very close to the southern wall of the Holy of Holies and within the entire Temple platform or compound.

On the other hand, we are in the twentieth chapter of a Lucan story that is twenty-four chapters long; we are near the end of the story. Particularly from Chapter 9 onwards we have been warned often that, once Jesus reaches Jerusalem, he will die (and rise). We are then well prepared to meet the opposition of certain Jews in authority, and are ready for a hostile environment and then the final arguments that will culminate in the crucifixion (and resurrection) of Jesus.

Literarily, then, we are within the tensions of a mortal combat. Jesus will prove himself unwilling to stop preaching his understanding of his Father's will, and authorities will not back down from their insistence that he is wrong, he is misleading the people - and deserving of death for that (cf. Deut, 13, 1-5, particularly: "That prophet or dreamer must be put to death, because he preached rebellion against the Lord your God...he has tried to turn you from the way the Lord your God commanded you to follow. You must purge the evil from among you"). It is within this difficult atmosphere that our parable is recounted. Indeed, it is evident that by this parable Jesus means to interpret for his enemies what Jesus understands their end will be — and then instruct what his own real end will be.

Symbolism and a point of Law

Symbolism

The Old Testament witnesses to the fact that for centuries Israel has been referred to as a 'vineyard'; very famous is the description from Isaiah, 5, 1-7, in which we read both a parable about a vineyard and a prophecy about Israel, the vineyard. In these Isaian verses, the prophet clearly identifies God as the one who planted and assiduously cared for this vineyard; it is His — to enjoy its fruit or to destroy its fruitlessness.

The parable is concerned with the vineyard workers, particularly with their cooperation with the owner of the vineyard. We find that the latter has entrusted his vineyard to his workers, then takes up a residence elsewhere for a long period of time; it is during this time that the owner will send a servant to collect the value of the grape harvests. What, the story asks, will the vineyard workers do with this request? We should note in passing that many writers of Luke's time use the number 3 in fictitious stories or parables; this certainly is a structural characteristic of Lucan parables.

The circumstances

The story tells us that three servants have been mistreated, humiliated and physically punished; all this in return for their request for the fruits which belong not to the workers but to their master. Since fruit of the vineyard is a common Old Testament theme standing for moral acts according to the Law of Moses, Jesus' audience can easily understand that Jesus means here that God is not receiving the good deeds He expects. One recognizes in our parable that the presence of three servants is a symbol of the long procession of prophets of the Old Testament who called for good deeds.

Particularly, and most important for us, they called on the leadership of Israel to guide the nation to good deeds. Our parable focuses on the particular and lasting Old Testament problem: the refusal of Israel's leaders to lead the people properly; inevitably this led to the people's disobedience — in parabolic terms, these leaders, by their actions and words, led the People to refuse the fruits of the vineyard to the owner. The Old Testament and our parable agree in this, that those who refused to listen to the prophets, who are here symbolized by the master's servants, now merit punishment; they agree in their condemning those who, while responsible for the spiritual health of Israel, prove themselves irresponsible. (Note that though the parable suggests that the motive of the vineyard workers is a takeover of the master's vineyard, this element is not applicable to real life; what is applicable is that these workers refused him the fruits of the vineyard he deserved.)

The monologue

At this point in the story Jesus presents us with a monologue; it is the owner of the vineyard speaking to himself. After mulling over matters he makes a decision: he will send no more servants, he will send his son. The thinking of the master might marginally appear prudent within the fictitious story, but it really verges on naiveté, once one realizes that the parabolic image here is to represent the relationship between Jewish leadership in Jerusalem and Jesus, Son of God. "They will surely respect my son." Perhaps the vineyard owner thinks so naively; could God think this way?

The son

The owner sends his son, his beloved. One realizes that Jesus is meant here, for in the Gospel he has already twice been called precisely 'the beloved'. We first read this description in Luke 3, 22: "You are my son, my beloved son...", and then in Luke 9, 35: "This is my son, my beloved son..." In both moments it is God who is describing Jesus with an emphasis through repetition: My son, My beloved son. God has already revealed that Jesus is divine (cf. the angelic message to Mary, Luke 1, 35). By this particular term 'beloved', God while recognizing the divinity of Jesus, means to say that He the Father has confidence in the Son's obedience, that Jesus will act as a son to his father. We are not to miss the thought of the parable that the sending of the son is a final attempt, and that it means to accomplish what the servants could not. We have here a step God takes beyond all that has occurred in Israel' history: not a prophet, but God's Son will come to urge the Jewish's leadership, and all Israel with them, to render to God the moral fruits of his vineyard, Israel.

With the passing of each servant, the vineyard workers prove all the more intransigent. One senses a climax building in the mind of the vineyard-owner; for him there can only be one outcome of this rebellious, unjust stance: the tragic destruction of the vineyard workers who killed the master's son. Then the master will have to find others who will give the fruits of the vineyard to its owner.

Finally, the fate of the son in the parable is that "Having thrown him out of the vineyard, they killed him". Luke clearly anticipates the killing of Jesus, through the urging of certain Jewish authorities, outside the city walls of Jerusalem. It is interesting to note that the parable does not run exactly as Mark has it. Luke's source, Mark, said that the son would be killed and then thrown out of the vineyard. Both Mark and Luke anticipate at this moment the death of Jesus, but Luke sharpens the sequence of "throwing out" and "killing" to reflect what will actually be the order of events: Jesus is led to Golgotha, outside the city, and then killed.

A point of law — Palestinian custom

The son of the vineyard owner is identified by the vineyard workers as 'the inheritor', and on the basis of this identification they think they should kill him. What is at the root of this thinking is custom which has become for many the equivalent of law. This custom of Israel stated that, if the sole son of an absentee landlord were to die, the workers of the vineyard would have first claim to own the vineyard. Notice that there must be no other son to whom the master could leave his inheritance and that the owner must be absent for long periods of time. This legality makes sense of the logic which underpins Jesus' story.

The son, then, is revealed in the parable as the only son. The audience of Luke can see clearly to whom Jesus refers in reality when he speaks about a 'son, a beloved and only son' and to whom the workers refer when they speak of the 'inheritor'.

The response to the parable

Jesus (at v. 9) addressed his parable to the people of Israel (a more formal term, filled with Jewish history, and not to just a 'crowd'). Near the end (v. 15b) of his recitation of this fictitious story he asks this people, "What do you think the owner of the vineyard will do (after his son's murder)"? With v. 16 Jesus answers his own question with the return of the vineyard owner to kill the rebellious vineyard workers.

The response to this is brief, but so poignant and baleful: "Oh, no!" or "Let it not be!"

The context of the parable

As noted earlier, this parable about the vineyard owner occurs on one of the days on which Jesus was teaching in the Temple area; the entrance of Jesus into the Holy City has already been positively described: "Blessed is he who comes in the name of the Lord"! Apparently, many people are on his side. Once Jesus has entered the city, he proceeds to the Temple, where he performs the prophetic act of driving out those selling things there (e.g. one bought there, and nowhere else, sheep or doves for an offering to Yahweh), arguing that these sellers make the Temple of God a cave of thieves, whereas it is the place of prayer. This gesture, Luke notes immediately, stirs up the desire of the Chief Priests and Scribes (who oversee this selling) to have Jesus killed.

There are a number of choices Luke has in describing Jesus' days in Jerusalem, before his Last Supper. He chooses seven stories, and follows those by the lengthy discourse on the tragic future of Jerusalem and thereafter. Of the seven stories, six have as their basis a challenge from Jerusalem authorities to the authority of Jesus or a criticism from Jesus about the scribes and 'those who give less than their all to God'. In the flow of things, the triumphal approach of Jesus to Jerusalem brings him to confront the abuse of the sellers on the Temple platform, which in turn leads to a challenge to his authority. This challenge is answered, first in a stand-off between the combatants, and then in Jesus' recitation of our parable about the fate of the Jewish leaders 'who refuse to listen to the son'. The saga of Jesus' teaching in the Temple area continues, then, with further challenges, to end with Jesus' challenge to the authorities: "How can it be that the Christ is the son of David?" No one of the authorities could answer that question; with that silencing Luke brings to an end the various challenges to Jesus' authority that Luke thought should be in his Gospel.

Given this acrimonious and continual attack on Jesus, we see better why our parable has as its subject, not the vineyard/the people of

Israel, but the vineyard workers/those responsible, through their teaching and proper Temple worship, for the holiness in Israel. It is within the constant battle between Jesus and the authorities that the parable finds its fullest meaning.

The full meaning of the parable

The vineyard workers are punished for their refusal to hear the just call of the vineyard owner; these workers had refused to obey. At earlier times, they had beaten, humiliated or wounded servants of the vineyard master; lastly, they killed his son, his beloved and only son. Crimes though these were, the central point of the parable looks to one 'relationship', that of the owner and the workers of his vineyard. Only later will this parable blossom into a statement about the victory of the son, the beloved and only son, over his enemies.

While one understands that Jesus preaches repentance to all people in Israel, and a number of his parables speak to this universal repentance, this particular parable focuses on the leaders of Israel and their refusal to aid in developing the spiritual good deeds of Israel — which is a refusal to aid in the development of the spirituality of the people of God. That the leadership of Jerusalem is the particular object of this parable is made very clear at the end: "The scribes and the chief priests tried to lay hands on Him ... for they understood that He spoke this parable against them" (v. 19). In a way, with this parable Luke lays at least partial groundwork for the upcoming speech of Jesus which will include a description of the tragic destruction of rebellious Jerusalem.

Very often the parables of Jesus have, in differing measures, an element of joy, something uplifting. In this parable there is only destruction, by both the central parties of the story. The story is intentionally threatening, with unrelenting punishment as its conclusion for refusal to hear God.

Of course, one is not dealing here with 'little sins'; here we read of murder, and of the murder of that person whom faith knows to be the only Son of God. When we move from parable to reality, we move from the fiction of a dispute between workers and their master to the real and terrible results of refusing the prophets and now Jesus.

One of the questions that often results from the preaching of Jesus and of his disciples has to do with 'refusal'. That is, what is being refused to God by the refusal to accept Jesus? The answer is, in the end, twofold: one the one hand, one refuses to heed the word of Jesus (as the word of the prophets, too, went unheeded), and on the other hand, one refuses to believe that Jesus is the Son of God as described in Luke 1, 35 and the Messiah and Lord of Israel. These latter two titles, Messiah and Lord, will be the central affirmation of the first and defining preaching after Pentecost (Acts 2). Jesus preached obedience to God, which implicitly, but necessarily called for faith in himself as full of God's Spirit and God's wisdom, and the Gospels and the disciples of Jesus, with God always on their minds, preached faith in Jesus and obedience to him. In the New Testament both objects of obedience — obedience to the words about morals and obedience which is faith in the identity of Jesus — belong together. As Jesus said, 'it is on the rock-solidness of my word that morality is built'. His word is right and worthy of esteem because of who he is: he is Son of God.

Further images

A. *The audience*

When Jesus speaks somberly of the punishments of Jerusalem's Jewish leadership, we hear the very human gasp of his audience, "Let it not happen!" The crowd has understood very well to whom the fictitious vineyard workers and vineyard owner refer; they, who so recently acknowledged Jesus to be king, align the attacks against Jesus with the historic attacks against God's prophets — Jesus' treatment is theirs. Theirs are the final words of this part of Jesus' story.

B. *The image of the spurned stone*

At this point, the parable of the disobedient vineyard workers comes to an end. But Jesus' words do not. He will not stop with the terrible end both he and his enemies must suffer. We can say that, given all his words in the Gospel, he can only continue on to speak of his resurrection from the death that will be imposed on him.

Jesus continues with the characters of the parable: God, Jesus, and many members of the Jerusalem Jewish leadership.

The image

Jesus fixes his stare at the crowds. How can you say "Let it not happen!"? But now, apart from his condemnatory remarks about the vineyard workers, he moves to another, but allied topic; surely you know the sacred words of the Psalmist: "The stone spurned by the builders has been made the corner stone (or cap stone)". With this image, Jesus builds on his prophecy that he would die at the hands of the Jerusalem leadership, to assert in this new image the event subsequent to his death, his resurrection from the dead. He will refer in a moment to the people who will not accept him, but for now he focuses on the complete story of the son of the vineyard owner. Indeed, Jesus applies to himself the imagery given in the prophetic words of Psalm 118, 22, and thereby indicates that the Old Testament is seen to anticipate, even if murkily, the death and resurrection of Jesus.

We are to imagine a building being built with stone. Certainly one of the most important decisions in the construction of a building is to make sure the walls are properly aligned so that the building will remain standing. The citation of Jesus supposes concern about two external, weight-bearing walls joined together at a 45° angle. The key to fitting these two conjoined walls correctly is the placement of a powerful stone at the corner where the two walls meet each other. Once that stone is solidly set in place, one has a guide to the placement of every other stone, of one wall and of the other — both in relation to length and width of the walls developed from that corner stone. Not only is that true of building walls outward from the corner — it is also true for placing the subsequent rows of stones to reach the desired height of the walls. In short, this image of the Psalmist, used now by Jesus, points to the extreme importance of this corner stone responsible for the solidity of an entire edifice. Should it not be placed right, the walls will be aligned imperfectly, all will fail; should the stone be placed correctly, all will succeed.

Sometimes, a translation of these words of the Psalm speaks not of the 'cornerstone', but of the 'capstone'. This image of the capstone points to another building moment, i.e. the building of an arch. The point at issue is why does not an arch, which has nothing to hold it up, fall? The arch begins from one solid wall at one end and closes upon another solid wall at the other end of the arch, but has nothing holding up its middle point. An arch can remain aloft because of the pressures exerted from both arms of the arch, one arm against another. BUT the key to holding these arms together, in such wise that the arms do not collapse for lack of support, is the capstone, that stone which is the middle stone of the arch, and the stone which mediates the pressure of each arm against the other and keeps the pressure such that the arch will not collapse. If that capstone cannot accept the pressures coming from either side of it, and so cannot transmit the pressures of the arms one against the other and thus keep each arm aloft, the one pressing hard against another — that is, if the middle or capstone cannot last, everything falls.

In either case, that of the corner stone or that of the capstone, the wise builder looks carefully for the right stone, all so that his building efforts will be a success. Thus, many stones can be discarded as one searches for just the right stone, the one that will sustain an entire building or arch.

In this building image the Psalmist proposes the 'impossible': a stone rejected by the builders, those who should know stones best, has been made the cornerstone of an entire edifice (or capstone of an arch).

The reality

Jesus is the stone rejected by authoritative builders, specialists in building up Israel. Within this image of acceptance/rejection is the reality that Jesus is talking about the People of God. This People is' the building which needs a solid foundation', and he claims that he is that foundation. Again, we sense the claim that Jesus sees himself as divine, for in Israel's history, it has always been God alone who upholds Israel.

The main verb of this sentence of the Psalmist is 'has become', or better 'has been made'. The image of building here always implies that someone is active, finding and using the stone, and that the stone is passive and used by someone. The application of the prophecy to Jesus' situation is made by considering that the builders (no longer the vineyard workers — we have switched images and left them in favour of stone) are the ones who have rejected Jesus, the stone qualified to found God's People, but not accepted by Jewish leadership as such. Of course, implicit is the claim of Jesus that all his life should be interpreted as 'the good stone', not 'a stone to be rejected'. That the verb in this sentence is passive in form indicates that God will make the stone, Jesus, the cornerstone (capstone). Jesus will be raised from the dead by his Father. The verb in our prophecy also suggests a time sequence: first the builders reject the stone, then God makes it the corner- or capstone. It is from another point of consideration about Jesus that John's Gospel will quote Jesus as saying that Jesus will raise himself from the dead.

The idea of Jesus as raised from the dead as 'cornerstone' speaks to the reality very soon to come: after Jesus will be officially rejected by most all the authority of Jerusalem, he will be raised up by God to be the basis of the community of all disciples. As St Paul, when seeking the basis of unity among Christians, suggested many years before Luke, 'Who died for you, and in whose name were you baptized?', so now Luke for his part indicates through Psalm 118 that Jesus is the foundation stone rejected by the human authority, and then made by God to be the foundation of the Christian community. On Jesus 'will my church be built'.

C. The image of the hard stone

We have noted that the required stone has to be a most solid and powerful stone. It is not a stone which will crumble under the weight of others. Jesus now adds to the foundational aspect of the 'right stone' chosen by God this characteristic of the stone: it is hard, solid, unyielding. If the stone falls on someone, that someone will suffer; the stone will remain whole and solid. And if one falls upon it, it is the fallen one who suffers; the stone remains unfazed and solid.

Luke had much earlier recounted the words of Simeon (2, 34): "This child is destined for the falling and the rising of many in Israel, and to be a sign that will be opposed". This is the one hint in the Infancy Narratives about a tragic refusal of Jesus. Luke 20, so close now to the time of the cross, is now sensitive to the rejection of Jesus and provides us with threatening and authoritative words and images of Jesus in this regard.

Conclusion

As indicated earlier, should there be any doubt about the object of Jesus' harsh teaching here, Luke makes it clear: "The scribes and the chief priests tried to lay hands on him at that very hour...for they perceived that he had told this parable against them" (20, 19). At this moment, Jesus speaks not about the response of people in general to his preaching and person, but of the response of authorities of Jerusalem; thus far, the responses of the crowds, though varied, never included the intention of violence towards Jesus — indeed, only once, at the trial before Pilate, and under the influence of a part of the leadership, does the people side against Jesus (23, 13-14). The leadership will meet a harsh end, the parable teaches. Moreover, no matter that they 'throw away this stone', God will raise up Jesus to be the foundation of the worshippers of God. Indeed, the strength of Jesus will outlast that of his opponents and they will stumble over him, not move him out of the way, and be 'crushed by him whom they tried to crush'.

CONCLUSION

Luke wrote his Gospel and Acts of the Apostles 'in order that Theophilus may know the reliability of the things he had been taught'. This overall purpose of the Lucan work is aided by three further considerations.

First, Jesus tells his audience (and so Luke tells his readers) that he must preach the good news, that is, the Kingdom of God: "It is necessary that I preach the good news, which is the kingdom of God; for this I was sent" [4, 43]). As the Gospel progresses, it becomes clear that this joyful announcement of the kingdom must include the fact that the kingdom is already here: "If I drive out demons by the finger of God, then the kingdom of God has come upon you" (11, 20). This presence of the kingdom is later affirmed: "Behold the kingdom of God is within you" (17, 21). alongside the proclamation that the kingdom is present is Jesus' affirmation to his disciples that it is in the future that the kingdom of God will come in its fullness, certainly after the destruction of Jerusalem and the completion of the days of the Gentiles (21, 24).

Second, essential to the announcement of the presence, nearness, and coming kingdom of God is Jesus' awareness of the subordinate purpose of his public life: "I have come to call sinners to repentance" (5, 32). This call is 'a mighty urging that people enter the kingdom' (16, 16).

Third, with Jesus' physical withdrawal from this world, the tasks which characterized Jesus' public life he now bestows upon his disciples. All they do as disciples fall under the heading of 'witness' ("You will be my witnesses in Jerusalem, in all of Judaea and Samaria, and to the end of the earth" [Acts 1, 8]). This 'witness' can take many forms, e.g. suffering, preaching, martyrdom, living the Christian life, performing miracles. All, however, is to further the major goal of Jesus, the announcement that the kingdom is present and to come, and the subordinate goal of Jesus, the call for repentance so as to enter that kingdom through the Final Judgment.

Within all that is said above are to be placed one of a variety of methods Jesus used to teach: the parable. All the parables, as means to an end, are to help people realize the presence and the future coming of the kingdom and to prepare to enter it. Certain aspects of repentance, as drawn from the parables, are particularly Lucan concerns; perhaps the most consistent theme he presents is that of the proper use of wealth, with his regard for the love of neighbor and the less fortunate, and its concern about the dangerous haughtiness and selfishness its misuse creates. Certainly, too, especially with Luke's knowledge of the 50 or so years between Jesus' departure and his writings, Luke is concerned with fidelity (at times joined with 'the faith'), fidelity under persecution, fidelity in prayer.

Parables have only a little to do with what will be a major Lucan preoccupation in his Acts, namely the entrance of the Gentiles into the kingdom as full members together with their Jewish brothers and sisters. There is no doubt that some parables speak about Gentiles coming to the kingdom, but they do so only to highlight the need now, in Jesus' lifetime, for repentance. Parables, because of their attractiveness, are marvellous forms of teaching — as is evident even today. Jesus was a master parablist. Luke appreciated the teachings of Jesus in parables; as Luke expanded the narrative of Jesus' journey to Jerusalem beyond Mark's narrative of the same journey, Luke filled that movement towards the Pascal Mystery with parables. It is to Luke's credit that he has saved for us so many parables, particularly two of the most famous parables of all, that of The Good Samaritan and that of the Prodigal Son. But then we know that it was the Spirit of God who preserved the parables of Jesus.

STAMPA: Settembre 2008

presso la tipografia
"Giovanni Olivieri" di E. Montefoschi
ROMA • info@tipografiaolivieri.it